Don't Put Your Dreams on Hold

Nathan F. Serota

Copyright 2001 by Nathan L. Serota

All rights reserved.

No part of this book may be reproduced or utilized in any form or by any means, electronic or mechanical, including photocopying, recording or by any information storage and retrieval system, without permission in writing from the Publisher.

Inquiries should be addressed to:
Biography for Everyone
105 N.E. 19 Avenue, #250
Deerfield Beach, FL   33441
800-393-KATE (5283) or 954-461-5283

Library of Congress Control Number: 2001 131236

ISBN 1-888069-14-7

Cover design by Caren Hackman

Printed in the United States of America

Dedication

To my beloved soul mate, Vivian.

That's Success

It's doing your job the best you can
And being just to your fellow man;
It's making money--but holding friends
And true to your aims and ends;
It's figuring how and learning why
And looking forward and thinking high
And dreaming a little and doing much.
It's keeping always in close touch
With what is finest in word and deed;
It's being thorough, yet making speed;
It's daring blithely the field of chance
While making labor a brave romance;
It's going onward despite defeat
And fighting staunchly, but keeping sweet;
It's being clean and it's playing fair;
It's laughing lightly at Dame Despair;
It's looking up at the stars above
And drinking deeply of life and love.
It's struggling on with the will to win
But taking loss with a cheerful grin;
It's sharing sorrow and work and mirth
And making better this good old Earth;
It's serving, striving through strain and stress;
It's doing your noblest--That's Success!

Berton Braley

Table of Contents

1 "Where To, Mr. Scrota?" 1

2 Maternal Grandparents 3

3 Paternal Grandparents 5

4 Father and Mother 9

5 Childhood Snapshots of Family Life 13

6 School Days 19

7 The Ice Plant and the Coal Yard 23

8 Finances on Track at the Pennsylvania Railroad 31

9 The Army 37

10 First Furlough, Getting Married 43

11 Fay 47

12 Making Money as Number A59 51

13 To All The Girls I've Loved Before 55

14 Changing Fortunes 63

15 Married Life, Children, and Building a Business 67

16 Family Life 73

17 Partnership: From Residential to Commercial 77

18 The Auction 87

19 Enjoying the Battle 93

20 My Love, Vivian . . . and Marrying Her 97

Forword by Cheryl Lee Terry 97

21	Life With Vivian and the Children	107
22	Economic Hard Times	115
23	Fighting the "Boys"	121
24	Grand Jury, the Trial and Appeal	127
25	You Never Know Who Your Friends Are	133
26	Health Interests	137
	Introduction by friends, Arnold and Anne Kopelson:	137
27	Involvement With Daytop Village	145
28	Chauffeur, Secretary, and Other Fine Employees	149
29	Close Calls With the Cops	155
30	You Can Win a Race, But You Can't Beat the Races	159
31	Fay's Death	163
32	Believe in Yourself	165

33 Work or Play, I Enjoyed Every Day **169**

34 Why is My Tombstone in My Office? **173**

Obituary for Nathan L. Serota 175

35 Secrets of a Good Marriage **177**

36 Children and Grandchildren **181**

37 The World According to Serota **183**

38 Final Thoughts **189**

Foreword

"DON'T PUT YOUR DREAMS ON HOLD"

I often printed the above motto in big letters and gave it to friends. Sometimes it hung over my desk, and throughout my life, it remained in my mind to guide and inspire me.

Over a year ago, after I recovered from a serious illness, my wife, Vivian, talked to me with determination about her idea of publishing my stories. "God forbid anything happens to you, Nat," she said. "You've two granddaughters who know you well because they're twenty and twenty-three, but your grandsons' ages range from eighteen months to nine years, and they will hardly remember you. Those five boys and the generations to come should know who their grandfather or their great-grandfather was. I really think you should write a book, and I'm going to find somebody to help you do it."

Vivian found this wonderful lady, Kate Winters and Biography for Everyone who wove a written tapestry from my spoken words. You're holding the result in your hands.

This is not meant to be a complete documentary, and I do not intend to hurt feelings by not mentioning someone. My wife asked me to write my life story--not an autobiography, not even a memoir really--just true stories. As people learned what we were doing, many had suggestions about what I should write. My apologies to those who thought their names should get in my book; write your own damn book!

At first I had no use for the idea, but as I worked on this project, it became clear to me that there was something I needed to say; there was a message I wanted to leave for my loved ones. Through sharing my story, I want to show that anyone can make it by believing in themselves and never giving up. This book is for you. **DON'T PUT YOUR DREAMS ON HOLD.**

Nathan L. Serota
New York, Summer 2001

Acknowledgments

I thank my beautiful and lovely wife, Vivian, for getting me to record these stories. During the Millennium New Year, I fell and awoke ten days later in a hospital bed, giving Vivian cause for concern. Some time before, she'd suggested I write a book about all the stories I tell at dinner parties, but I'd been too busy for that. Now I had to sit still in Florida for more than a month, and she thought telling my stories would be a stress-free activity to keep me busy while I recovered. So, to make a long story short . . . I sat still and told my stories.

I thank *Biography for Everyone*, for the many hours of planning, transcribing, writing, and editing, and for all the suggestions given to make my stories come alive on these pages. Thank you to all the team members who helped me: the delightful, easy-to-get-along-with Kate Winters, owner and chief editor; Margaret Fraser, writer; Caren Hackman, graphic artist and designer; and the transcribers and copy editors who made this book possible.

Thanks to the six gifted doctors who have helped me reach my eighty-second year: Dr. Michael Wolk, Dr. Lawrence Cohn, Dr. Seth Baum, Dr. Jay Schapira, Dr. Wayne Isom, and Dr. David Guyer.

I thank Arnold Kopelson for taking my photo on the dust cover.

And last, if I'd mentioned all of our friends in the States who have added so much to our lives, this book would have been 1,000 pages long. I thank you all, even though your names may not appear on these pages.

First Introduction: Buzz Aldrin

When Nat and I first met, we connected instantly. He's a down-to-earth, straight-talking guy. The day after our first meeting, while we were vacationing in Monte Carlo, he asked me and Lois to join him and his wife for a sail and a swim. Unfortunately, we had already accepted an invitation to have lunch on someone else's yacht, so at first I had to pass. But Nat was quick to offer a tempting incentive to help me change my mind. He said: "That's okay. Just remember that I have a day boat--whenever you want, you can join me for a visit to the "naked beach" at Cap d'Ai!"

Clearly, this invitation had a lot more to offer than a mere lunch, so I quickly changed my plans. Once we got there, we found that no one was willing to go into the water, which was filled with jellyfish. But Nat was as fearless as I am--he jumped right in. The women on the beach were attractive, certainly, but it was Vivian who kept Nat's attention. He only had eyes for her, as she lay on the deck looking lovely and enjoying the hot sun.

That's when I learned about Nat's great sense of humor. Here was this guy, no spring chicken, surrounded by a beach full of muscle-bound types, and he had no self-consciousness--even better, his ability to laugh at himself allowed him to swagger along the beach with as much panache as any of those buff young beach boys. That vacation cemented what has become a lifelong friendship. Whenever I'm in New York, Nat's the first friend I call.

-Buzz Aldrin
Apollo II Astronaut
Walked on the moon July 20, 1969

Second Introduction: Marshall Feldstein

Nat Serota and I have never done business together because I know him too well; I know what a pain in the ass he can be. We were neighbors, lived right around the corner from each other in New York City. In 1980, Nat's wife, Vivian, and my wife, Diane, met at a surprise party for a mutual friend and bonded immediately. The next thing I knew we were invited to a dinner party at the Serota's.

They had a gorgeous apartment on 79th Street. That first evening we spent together was totally pleasant--excellent dinner with a group of interesting guests and a talented pianist. The conversation flowed easily, until all of a sudden, as the evening started to draw to a conclusion, Nat rose from his chair and announced, "Okay, that's it. Everybody get the hell out of here. I'm tired and it's time for me to go to bed."

That was my first introduction to the charming social graces of Nathan Serota.

As I walked home, I wondered what kind of guy would invite people to his home for dinner, then throw them out. I couldn't figure this man out. Obviously, he must be doing all right since he lived in a wonderful apartment with a beautiful, charming wife. I didn't realize it then, but that first meeting was full of insight into who Nat really is. He speaks what's on his mind and does whatever he thinks is appropriate. What anyone else thinks or what social graces society calls for are immaterial to Nat Serota.

Although Nat and I were both in business, we had little in common business-wise. The friendship grew as Diane and I started to spend more and more time with the Serotas socially. I found myself enjoying Nat's company: we compared notes on our respective business ventures and discussed the usual subjects men talk about. He is a true individual and a very bright guy to talk with.

What ultimately gave me the greatest insight into Nat Serota was spending three weeks traveling in the Orient with him. Our wives planned this terrific vacation for the four of us. There wasn't a soul we told about this trip who thought we'd all be talking to one another when it was over. In three weeks we visited China, Thailand, Hong Kong, and Japan, and during that time, the four of us were rarely apart. Interestingly enough, after three weeks of spending so much time together, the first thing we did upon returning to New York was meet for breakfast at the local coffee shop on our block to reminisce about our fabulous trip. We had a lot of fun and did some crazy, silly things; the craziest and silliest were, of course, done by Nat.

My wife was in the public relations business and had arranged for us to have a van with a driver in China, as well as an interpreter. The driver spoke no English. One day, he drove us to see the Great Wall, and on the return trip we had an accident. A little boy of about three or four years old walked beside the road holding the hand of an elderly, typically bearded, Chinese man who was his grandfather. Suddenly, the boy let go of his grandfather's hand and darted across the road, directly into the path of our van! The child was hit, but fortunately, not badly hurt. It was very upsetting to everybody. Our driver immediately stopped the van in the middle of the road, cutting off traffic going both ways, and jumped out. He accompanied the boy and his grandfather to the hospital, and was gone for about an hour. (Apparently, that was the rule when you hit someone.)

So, there we were: four Americans stuck in a van in rural China, between Beijing and the Great Wall, completely blocking traffic. The road was lined sporadically with private homes and some factories, but this wasn't like the U.S. where everyone has private cars (most of the Chinese rode bicycles). Lots of trucks, carrying soldiers and workers, started to pile up on either side of us, waiting to pass. The area didn't appear heavily populated, but seemingly out of nowhere, hundreds of people surrounded us, chattering in Chinese. It was very scary, very tense--exactly the kind of thing that moved Nat Serota to action.

No help at all, our guide was completely intimidated by the whole event. He insisted we had to stay put and wait for the driver to return. "Don't move the car! The police, soldiers, the military will come," he told us fearfully.

As Nat opened the door, intending to get out and climb into the driver's seat to move the car, I said, "You're crazy. Don't do it! Just get back in the car where you belong and wait for this thing to settle down."

"The hell with it. I'll do what I damn want. Nobody can pass us in either direction. I've got to move this car out of the way." He parked the van on the side of the road, then proceeded to stand beside it and direct traffic like a policeman on the corner of 42nd and Fifth Avenue in downtown New York. The absurdity of the whole thing was that everybody paid attention to him as if he knew what the devil he was doing. Nat was totally in charge.

Suddenly, a five star general with more braid on his uniform than you can imagine drove up on his motorcycle with a side car. Oh no, now we're in real trouble, I thought. It was a hot summer day, and Nat was dressed in light white trousers and a white shirt, contrary to the Chinese who wore heavy-looking dusty browns and grays. He looked very much a foreigner, very white. But the general simply obeyed Nat's direction and drove on by. It was mind-boggling--really, very funny. Even though he was halfway around the world in a country where he didn't speak the language, Nat was still the same take-charge guy.

We stayed at the Sheraton Great Wall, the only Western hotel in Beijing at the time. The first day there we visited an Oriental temple nearby, a big tourist attraction. There were a hundred wide steps leading up to an ornate front door (like the Capitol of America). The temple was an impressive sight, very grand.

As we were leaving the temple, Nat and I decided to visit the restroom. Now we're talking primitive facilities here, mere holes in the ground. (Thinking of this story still makes me laugh.) When we entered the room, we saw a man squatting--he was the most decorated soldier we'd ever seen in our lives: braid, medals, epaulets and all kinds of things on his uniform--without his pants, his testicles dangling over the hole. In amazement, I looked at Nat. Without batting an eyelash, he took out his camera and snapped a picture of this guy. I tell you, I wanted to die. Any moment I expected the military to surround us right there.

We hurried outside, and I don't remember ever laughing so much in my life. I mean, I was convulsing. We didn't stop laughing for a couple of hours. It was a hilarious example of what makes Nat Serota tick. He has more brass than anyone I've ever known.

Typically, Nat went overboard with shopping, but even more so in the Orient because everything was so lovely and inexpensive. One day, we walked into the famous Friendship store, the only place to buy things in China at that time. Diane and I looked around, then quietly bought six or eight beautiful cloisonné bracelets. Nat created a mob scene by saying, "I want to buy every piece in the whole department!" He cleared out the entire department and created a riot in the store when other tourists ran over to see what was happening.

At another shop, he found lacquered Chinese doors, intricately carved in red and gold, and asked the manager to wrap up all twelve doors and ship them to America. That was Nat's way of doing business. No matter what, it was "I'll take them all."

Another time, we were crawling around on the second floor of a retail store in China, and there Diane and I uncovered three or four gorgeous urns, four feet tall and very large. Nat asked the proprietor how many they had. He bought the whole damn lot--twenty or thirty of these huge urns--and had them all packed and shipped. The same thing happened in Japan with some lovely Oriental kimonos, big heavy robes with all kinds of brocade and decoration. And in Hong Kong, Nat must have bought another two thousand cloisonné bracelets. At the time, I thought I was buying a lot, but I brought home a pittance compared to Nat. He brought home half a ship load from that three-week trip to the Orient.

There is another side to Nat Serota that people often don't see, an antithetical side to all his brash "I'll-buy-it-all--no fear, do-whatever-it-takes--take-charge" demeanor. Nat has a gentler, little boy side which is also very much a part of who he is. To illustrate this I'll tell you another story from our trip.

We met a gentleman in Bangkok through a friend of Vivian's. A very successful businessman in an incredible way, this man was a major supplier of rubber bands to the U.S. Post Office. Also very hospitable, his delight in life was showing tourists around Bangkok; he loved to entertain people who visited his country. Every morning, he picked us up in his yellow Cadillac and toured us around.

When I asked him what was the biggest tourist attraction in Bangkok, he suggested Nat and I visit "the baths, these wonderful baths with a VIP section," he explained. Our wives encouraged us to go and see what it was all about. One day, we left them for the baths at one o'clock in the afternoon. "You'll probably be back by two," Diane and Vivian said. We were there all afternoon and didn't return to the hotel until after five!

It really was an elegant place. The third floor was the important floor, the VIP area. The main room on the third floor resembled a gracious living room or parlor where soft music played and drinks were served by tuxedo-clad gentlemen who introduced us to the girls. There were at least forty lovely, delicate, young women to choose from, all dressed to perfection in gorgeous Oriental gowns, their hair and makeup beautifully done.

Nat and I each picked out a girl who caught our fancy. The baths in Bangkok were more civilized than a house of prostitution. You have a drink, some food if you want, then the girls give you a bath. The bathtubs, actually made by American Standard, are the size of a room--fourteen feet by ten feet. It's not a bad day, being scrubbed and massaged in a giant bathtub by a soft-skinned beauty.

When I came out of my bath, Nat was already out of his. I found him sitting on a couch with this tiny, round-faced girl who couldn't have been more than twenty years old. Nat looked as nervous as a freshman in high school at the senior prom. He jumped up. "Marshall, I want to introduce you to Toy," he said eagerly, like a little boy on his first date. It was the funniest thing I'd ever seen, and such a dichotomy to the Nat Serota people usually saw.

"What's your girl's name?" Nat asked me.

I admitted I didn't know, hadn't thought to ask.

He stared at me in wonder. "You just spent three hours with her and you don't know her name! My Toy spoke English. She did," he added with a shy grin.

I learned something important about Nat Serota that day. Under all his brash, take-charge attitude, the man has a soft center, a gentle, caring heart. Through this book, I hope you will enjoy knowing him as much as I do.

Marshall Feldstein
New York, NY

. . . . a word from Nat:

Marshall, the above story explains it all, and I just want to add that you and Diane are dear to my heart and I treasure your friendship. Diane, please stop waking me up every morning at 8:00 to speak to Vivian . . . .

Don't Put Your Dreams on Hold

Nathan L. Serota

1

"Where To, Mr. Serota?"

It was just another typical day. The car phone wouldn't shut up and my chauffeur wouldn't drive fast enough.

"Step on it, Tom. I'm late!" I yelled.

Tom Cambria smiled calmly as if he had secret knowledge that everything was right with the world because his boss was yelling. It was when I didn't yell that he thought something was wrong. He pulled the 1965 James Young Rolls Royce limousine away from the curb and slid smoothly into the frantic stream of New York City traffic, taking his own sweet time as usual. I knew he'd drive at his own pace no matter what I said or how much I yelled.

The damn phone rang again and I reached for it.

"Talk fast," I barked. "I don't have a lot of time." I listened briefly to the details of another deal, then cut the speaker off.

"Offer him a million two," I said, "and no more!" I listened for a few seconds longer to the mixture of excitement and frustration in the negotiator's voice on the other end of the line before I disconnected.

I tried to settle back into the soft leather seat, then leaned forward. "Can't you drive this God-damned thing any faster?" Tom nodded to me in the rearview mirror while continuing to drive carefully under the speed limit like a new student in a drivers' ed class.

The cell phone rang again.

"Talk fast," was my standard greeting, then I quickly answered the contractor's query. "No, the deal was for two hundred thousand, no extras. What are you, deaf?"

I clicked off the phone and glanced out the window to see we were moving agonizingly slowly, packed in the middle of the sea of traffic funneling onto the George Washington Bridge. So, now what? For some reason, today I hadn't brought my usual pile of paperwork along. The phone was blessedly quiet, and I'd be damned if I'd voluntarily get on it right now, even to call my lovely wife. For this moment in time there was nothing I could do but sit back and look out at the beauty of the Hudson River and remember . . . .

Life hadn't always been this way. I remember a time, which seemed not so long ago, when cell phones didn't exist. Hell, I remember a time when *traffic in New York City* hardly existed.

There was a time when my grandfather supplied heavy hardware from his store to boats going up and down this very river. I remember a time of working hard and taking risks. And I remember the mouth watering smells of my mother's cooking every Friday evening when my whole family gathered for dinner at our house.

To make a long story short . . . .

2

Maternal Grandparents

In Brooklyn, when I was young, my mother's parents, Judah and Esther Bier, lived a few minutes away from us. Every Friday night, without fail, my grandparents, my parents and most of the extended family got together to have dinner. Friday evenings were always large, noisy family affairs featuring lots of scrumptious Kosher food: gefilte fish, chopped liver, fricassee, soup, chicken, and a great variety of cakes and deserts.

After dinner the adults played Pinochle which was, I think, their major joy. While the adults played, the kids ran around all over the place, making too much noise and interrupting the game. We were repeatedly told to go in the other room or we'd get whacked (and sometimes we did). My mother was the eldest of ten children--three boys and seven girls--so I had plenty of aunts and uncles and lots of cousins to play with.

Grandfather Bier always dressed neatly in a suit and tie. He looks big in photographs, but he was a small man with brown hair, sideburns and a mustache. A devoutly religious man, he went to the synagogue to pray almost every morning. He owned *Judah Bier's Hardware*, a very successful store on Grand Street in Manhattan which carried heavy hardware important to the area at that time. He supplied special goods for the many boats on the East River, railroad pieces, heavy tools, motor parts for ships, and everything necessary for large vehicles and other equipment along the river.

My grandfather was a gentle, charming man who loved to garden. He turned the whole backyard of their home on 64th Street into a vineyard. He grew concord grape vines on lattice, the same type of grapes some wine companies use today, and made his own wine. One of his daughters--my aunt, Nettie Bier--ran the hardware store with my grandfather. During the blizzard of 1888, he was hit by a snowball that broke his eardrum and made him deaf. After that, he didn't get to the store as often as he should have, but he still went to the temple every day.

My grandmother, Esther Bier, was a nice looking woman with red hair. She took good care of her ten children and their home in Brooklyn. In those days, the kids used to sleep two or three to a room. My grandmother was a homebody, and the only thing she did to have fun was play Pinochle with my grandfather and some of their friends and relatives.

One thing I remember about my grandmother is that she always had coffee and hot milk on the stove. When the milk was kept warm, it developed a skin on top. My mother and my grandmother always drank a lot of coffee, a tremendous amount. I never drink coffee, and these days, most people don't drink as much coffee as they did in my grandmother's day.

3

Paternal Grandparents

My father's parents both died before I was born on February 10, 1920. I was named after my grandfather, Nathan Serota. It is a Jewish tradition to name someone after a relative who died rather than after someone living, and I was no exception.

The Serotas immigrated from Russia when my father was six years old. They weren't allowed to come directly to the United States, so originally they went to Argentina and later sneaked into the country through New Orleans, then settled in New York. In my mind, immigrants like my grandparents were successful because they showed their children how to work hard and earn a living by example. It was a struggle for them to get enough money just to feed their families. They developed their education, studied a new language and culture, and built character through the challenge of making a new life. Today, it's still a challenge for poor immigrants and their children to succeed. They are the ones who work like hell to make something of themselves and, by doing so, develop a tenacious strength of character. That's what my family did.

My father, Charles Serota, knew what it was like to make a living as a child. At eight or nine years old he went to work with his family in a flour mill in New Orleans. I remember a story I was told about how he handled difficulties.

When he was young, his mother, Lena Serota, my grandmother, packed his lunch for work every day. And every day someone would steal his lunch. He finally told one of the men at the plant about this, and they plotted to catch the thief. In the flour mill, there were mice and rats running around, so they killed a rat, sliced it up and put it between the bread. The man who'd been stealing lunches never stole another one! And my father went on to become very successful at the plant.

My father was a builder, as was his father before him. My grandfather, Nathan Serota, died on the job at age forty-two. He had been building a temple in Brownsville, New York, which was mostly farm land then, over a hundred years ago. My grandfather was operated on for appendicitis. They didn't know a lot medically in those days, and he returned to work too soon, split open his appendix incision and bled to death.

My father was only sixteen at the time. Being the eldest of ten, he then became the family breadwinner and took over his father's business. His mother, I understand, was a tough and capable woman, well able to run the household while her son brought the money home. My father made a good living and went on to become a successful builder, all the while providing the money to raise his nine siblings. He had two sisters and seven brothers. While building his own business, Charles managed to send two of his brothers, Al and Leon, to college to become pharmacists.

My father talked his next oldest brother, Dave, into opening up first a coal yard and later an ice plant. He loaned him the startup money. Uncle Dave was very bright and, at that time, coal was an important commodity. Everybody heated their homes and businesses with coal; there were no oil furnaces then. The coal business became so promising that my father convinced Al and Leon to sell their pharmacies and give the proceeds to

Dave in order to buy into his coal yard. They did, and the three brothers became partners.

Shortly after that, there was a coal strike and nobody could get coal. The Serota brothers still had coal up to their ears, so naturally, they raised the price. One of their clients was the Koppers Coke Company, who, in those days, was as big as General Electric is today. Koppers Coke bought the Serotas' anthracite (hard coal) and put it through furnaces to extract the gas, then sold the gas. They didn't know what to do with the waste product (coke) which remained and used to dump it in the swamp. Coke was not solid and hard like anthracite, but soft, white chunks. My uncles thought it could be burned as fuel.

By that point, because of the strike, there was no anthracite or bituminous (soft coal) left to be had anywhere. Always alert for a new opportunity, the Serota brothers made a deal to buy the coke back from Koppers (who were going to dump it) for practically nothing, then sold it at huge profits to be used as fuel during the strike. They would ultimately become millionaires from their business successes in coal, oil, ice, and building.

Of the eight Serota brothers, one wasn't very bright and didn't make it. Sam went to jail for murder and eventually died of pneumonia after five years in Sing Sing. At the time, it was in the newspapers on a daily basis. My father visited him regularly in Sing Sing, but other than that, there wasn't much the family could do for Sam.

4

Father and Mother

I think one of the reasons my father died so young was because he kept everything inside, and it aggravated his body. Charles Serota was a very quiet man. Unlike myself, he would never have screamed or yelled. I yell like a crazy person, get it all out and forget it.

My father never learned to read or write, and he signed checks with an "X" for his name, but he built a successful business on his own, and at one time he was a millionaire, and that's a fact. He built apartment houses, commercial buildings and a lot of garages. He was always busy working, but he came home to his family every night.

My mother, Hannah Bier, was American-born and looked typically Irish, although her ancestry was from Russia. Her skin was very fair and her cheeks rosy. Even though she was still relatively young, my mother had completely white hair. (They didn't use hair dye in those days.)

She was the greatest cook in America. Every week she made *rugala*, a pastry made of special dough, rolled with jam, fruit, and nuts inside. Her other specialty was layer cake covered with chocolate or strawberries. She made everything from scratch, separating the eggs and beating the whites stiff.

Before my parents were married, my mother was considered an old maid at the age of twenty-six. My father was known as a confirmed bachelor, since he'd been in business for some years and raised his brothers and sisters. They met when someone told my father about an unmarried secretary who worked for William Chiles of Chiles Restaurants. Charles went to the restaurant and peered through the office window for a glimpse of Hannah, his future bride. They eventually went out on a date, fell in love and married.

By that time, my father was in his late thirties, and my mother was ten years younger. They had five children--boom, boom, boom--very close in age. The last one died at birth. My sister, Betty, was two years older than me (she passed away in 1999); my brother, Morton, is thirteen months my junior; my other sister, Rita, is two years younger than Morton.

My parents were both special people, but very opposite in temperament. Quiet and easygoing, my father would never fight. He didn't hit his children and didn't even spank any of us. My mother, on the other hand, was a real terror. She was the disciplinarian, the strong one.

My father suffered with hay fever and asthma. Every summer he came down with severe asthma and would have to go away to the White Mountains to escape the ragweed pollen. My mother then took over the job of building apartment houses--six-story buildings. My parents were a great team. Although a terror, my mother was as smart as a whip. While my father couldn't read or write, my mother's handwriting was elegant, like the old English script.

Some things about my parents were predictable and endearing. Every Saturday afternoon my father listened to his favorite radio program sponsored by General Motors. He loved to listen to the opera and turned the radio up loud, but nonetheless always wound up falling asleep in his chair. Annoyed, my mother would snap off the radio and my father would wake up with a start, wondering what happened.

My father used to make one barrel of wine per year in the basement of our home. I can see him now, proud of his wine, calling to my mother, "Hannah, try this. It's ripe; it's ready." She'd come downstairs and oblige him. Almost immediately her white skin turned bright red from her allergy to wine. She simply couldn't drink it.

Some say history repeats itself. Fortunes are won and lost. My grandfather died when my father was sixteen and my father had to take over the building business to support his family. My father died suddenly of a stroke at fifty-six, when I also was only sixteen.

In every business there are cycles. This was during the Depression, terrible economic times for the country and, therefore, the building business. My father rented buildings, but nobody had jobs, so people couldn't pay their rent. That meant he couldn't pay his mortgage on the buildings, and he ended up losing them all. The stress of these tough times surely contributed to his early death.

Poverty struck my family. We were completely broke and lost our house in Brooklyn. The bank let my mother and her four children live there for fifty dollars a month, with rent payable to Cruckink Mortgage which managed the property for the bank. The police delivered a fifteen dollar welfare check for my mother to feed us. In those days, a nickel bought a dozen eggs and a dime bought a pound of sugar.

5

Childhood Snapshots of Family Life

Since my father was a builder, we moved around a lot. At one time, we lived in a house on Empire Boulevard, a nice neighborhood in Brooklyn. There we had a dog, a white miniature poodle. With my father's business there were always painters around, and we always had paint. So, one day, my brother and I decided to paint the dog green.

I was a precocious child. My mother was a stern disciplinarian, and we were often at odds. My sister tells the story of when I was a little boy, three or four, and I stood on the porch calling all the workers passing the house "shitass" and other bad words. My mother tied me to a chair and washed my mouth out with soap.

Whenever I did something wrong (which was often), my mother beat the hell out of me. She'd tie me to a chair for punishment with a rope or a strap. My father was worried that someday she'd actually kill me. My father had built a whole row of houses on Carroll Street, and we lived in the big one on the corner. In the summer, when he went to Howard House in the White Mountains because of his asthma, he'd tell Hannah to please not kill *Nucham* (Jewish for Nathan) before he got home. Jewish children, in those days, were called by their Jewish baby names; for instance, my brother was Morton and he was called *Moishe*.

Once, when I was twelve, I had enough of my mother's form of discipline. Again, she beat the devil out of me for playing with some older boys whom she objected to, and I got very angry at her. When Hannah got through beating me I ran away from home.

I ran ten blocks away--to join the circus. Every year, on the old golf course (where the Brooklyn College is now), the Barnum and Bailey Circus pitched its tents for a week or ten days. From there, the circus traveled to Boston and then back to Madison Square Garden. I got a job right away at the circus watering elephants.

My mother went crazy, and when my father returned home, she told him, "Nucham disappeared. He ran away; he's gone!" They contacted all the friends I played ball with and asked them where I was. Nobody knew.

My stint with the circus didn't last long. They worried for two days until somebody finally found me there. I slept on the ground in the straw at the circus, and I slept very well. I really believe I could have handled that job and traveled with the circus, but my parents came and got me. My mother didn't hit me because she was so glad to see me and finally understood why I'd run away.

Hannah was hot stuff and one tough lady, but I loved her. I still say she was the finest cook in America. She cooked a tremendous amount of food on Fridays to last through the weekend. She made turkey, chicken, and steak (four nights a week), which eventually hurt my father's health. In those days, they knew little about nutrition and nothing about cholesterol and heart disease. Every morning before school my mother made us a different kind of hot cereal and poured heavy cream over it for breakfast. I ate hot cereal every day until I went to work at sixteen. Today, you couldn't pay me enough to eat hot cereal. I can't even look at it.

I used to help my mother bake bread. Out of the four kids, I was the best baker. Every Friday she made *challah* bread with yeast in it, the

Kosher way, braided and raised. There were chores every day after school. One of us had to clean the house, one of us did the cooking, one of us the mending, and the other the ironing. We rotated these jobs, and because of growing up in that family environment, we all learned how to take care of ourselves.

It is a wonder we developed any kindness in our hearts with the very stern mother we had. Despite being difficult, she had redeeming qualities. She took good care of us, fed us properly from morning to night, and taught us to value our education. I didn't appreciate it in childhood, but my mother taught me discipline and helped me to understand what life was all about. I needed discipline to accomplish the things I did later in my life.

My father and mother each had something unique to give us. My mother taught us the importance of education, and my father taught us to work. Although I never went to college, I did graduate from high school by finishing at nights. My brother, Morton, went to college and worked during the summers selling ice cream to put himself through after my father died. My sister, Betty, graduated from a lady's secretarial school. Rita, still a young child when my father died, later followed in Betty's footsteps and also graduated. When my father was building homes and apartment houses, Morton and I worked for him on the weekends. We'd take shovels and brooms and sweep out the new construction. We developed a work ethic and learned that nobody got anything for nothing.

Completely different from my mother, my father was a wonderful, calm man. He never got excited with any of us four kids. He taught me to be gentle, and how to listen to opera and appreciate music.

At one point, my father was a very wealthy man, but not always. Even though his business continually went up and down, he always provided his family with a nice place to live. The building business was (and still is) very erratic. My father would sometimes get into trouble and lose all his cash, then he had to sell off everything and start over again on a new building project. Looking back, I would say we moved eight to ten times in the first ten years of my childhood. We owned at least three or four different homes before I was eighteen, and each time we owned a house, it was because my father had built it.

Even when we were poor and had money problems, I always felt we were rich. As children we never lacked anything. We didn't have excess money, but we always felt we had what we needed. I still do. But you've got to get your ass out of bed and do something productive to make it in this world, and my father showed me that.

My father always had a big car. Once, he had a Coal car, a make of car most people have never heard of, a tremendous car with a twin gasoline engine. It had flappers on the side and no windows, just cellophane and material. My father drove well, but once he had a terrible accident on the Manhattan Bridge. The whole family was in the car, and we were traveling in the rain on a Saturday to go shopping for children's shoes for all four of us. The car went into a skid on the slippery bridge and hit another car, but thankfully, nobody was hurt. They probably had tow trucks then, but I don't remember what happened to our car after the accident. I do remember we all got our new shoes in the end.

At that time, we lived in a house on East 24th Street, and our next door neighbors were Peggy O'Malley, her husband, a New York City police detective, and her mother-in-law. Peggy had gorgeous red hair and freckles--a real dream boat. Her husband was about twelve years older than she was. I was fifteen and Peggy was in her mid-twenties; I was madly in love with her. I used to peek out my window to watch her, and sometimes I even talked to her. She was always nice to me. And every time I saw Peggy O'Malley, I loved her and wanted her more and more. If I knew then what I know now, I would have taken Peggy away.

But that was not to be. Peggy had problems with her mother-in-law, and the older woman eventually turned her son against his wife. The O'Malleys ended up divorced, but unfortunately for me, it was the detective and his mother who remained my neighbors. Peggy moved away to be with her father somewhere in upstate New York and broke my heart.

6

School Days

I was no genius in school and barely got through. I remember vividly not being able to spell and flunking on my report cards. When I was about eight or ten, I signed my own report card because it was so bad I was afraid to show it to my mother. At that time, we lived in our own big, beautiful home on East 24th, between Avenues "J" and "K" in Brooklyn (the middle section of Brooklyn was good then). My mother asked me where my report card was and I told her I didn't get one. She didn't believe me.

The following morning, when a classmate, Shirley Klein, came by the house to walk the six blocks to school with me, my mother asked if we'd had a report card. Shirley said we had. My mother marched into the school and got the report card I'd signed. She raised hell with my teacher, the beautiful blonde Mrs. Sears, for not noticing the difference in handwriting.

A tutor, Mrs. Liebermann, came to my house after school to teach me how to spell. She asked me, "How are you going to grow up and be in business without knowing how to spell?"

I told her I'd hire a secretary, of course. A secretary gets fifteen dollars a week to know these things. I didn't learn my lesson--either about spelling or about trying to get away with things--but I would later hire a great secretary.

Another teacher I remember fondly was Mrs. Applebaum. She was gorgeous and I loved her. The only reason Vivian is with me today is because she looked a lot like Mrs. Applebaum when she was younger. Well, maybe not the *only* reason, but that was my initial attraction to Vivian. Now, as I say this, I grin at my wife who comments that I always have an angle for everything. She's right, I do.

During my high school years, I had a job delivering newspapers in the afternoon. I swiped a bicycle because I needed one for the job. Well, you could say I borrowed it because I always gave it back. Sometimes I asked the person if it was okay to borrow the bike and sometimes I didn't. Sometimes I just took the damn thing, delivered my papers, then returned the bike. Since I worked in the afternoons, I didn't do my homework until the evening.

I was very active in sports. I liked to play ball or whatever was going on: ice skating, roller skating, hockey, football, basketball, baseball. My brother played too, but not as much as I did. We had close friends on the block that we played with. In Brooklyn, the avenue blocks ran about 1,000 feet, corner to corner (about five times the length of a short block). There were a lot of houses on a block that long, and everybody had kids, so I had a lot of friends. One was Bobby Brody, the best looking guy on the block. He and I would fight like hell because we both wanted to be the boss. For the two high school years I lived on that block, a bunch of us would regularly get together and play every type of game, and sometimes kids from other blocks would join us for a ball game. We had a lot of fun.

When I played sports in the street--hockey, football, basketball--I'd wear out the soles of my shoes every two weeks or so. One time, we were completely cash poor and my father complained about having to buy shoes for me. He said, "Nucham, you have to stop running and spending the money I don't have for new shoes every couple of weeks."

Shoes cost four to six dollars a pair in those days, and we shopped for

Coward shoes at the popular kids' shoe store called Thom McAnn. My mother was very conscious of us growing up with proper shoes that were good for our feet. I don't think we had particularly bad feet, but she was extra careful and took us to a specialist who custom-built arches for our shoes. This was typical of her.

Dating in high school was not anything special for me. I only dated casually because, in those days, a young man like myself didn't have sex with his dates. I had too much responsibility, being busy working and going to school. I had girl friends in high school, but just not in a dating situation.

My life changed drastically when my father had a stroke and died eleven hours later in April of 1936. I was just sixteen and had to quit school and leave my friends behind. I started working in the ice plant and the coal yard that my uncles owned. I had to be at the ice plant seven days a week, starting at six in the morning, and I finally finished my high school at nights.

My uncles were millionaires by that time, so I was puzzled by their lack of generosity when my father died. They didn't realize it then, when they hired me at the pitiful wage of two dollars a day, but they did me a real favor giving me the job of running the ice plant. Like many things in my life, I made the most of that opportunity. I was given a lot of responsibility and learned much about business during that time.

7

The Ice Plant and the Coal Yard

In April of 1936, I started working for Uncle Dave, Uncle Al, and Uncle Leon who were partners in the coal business and the ice plant. They wanted me to learn how to manage the ice plant right away. Making the ice was minor, but running the plant was another story.

The engineers worked shifts on a twenty-four hour basis to make sure the machinery at the ice plant was always running. It was a cold place to work, and I wore a jacket and gloves to keep warm. The ice was made under the floor in a machine which automatically produced the frozen blocks with hooks frozen into them. When the blocks were solid, the "box man" lifted the floor open, then picked up the blocks on the hooks frozen into them with an overhead machine and lifted them onto a conveyor belt. The blocks were a good three feet square by fourteen inches thick and weighed three hundred pounds each. A continuous line of machinery would deliver the blocks to the ice box, literally a frozen twenty thousand square foot warehouse constantly kept below thirty-two degrees to prevent the ice from melting.

When the trucks arrived to collect the ice and deliver it to our customers, the box man dropped the blocks on edge onto the conveyor belts, and the drivers picked them up by the hooks, snapping them up and loading their trucks practically in one smooth move. Each truck held fifty-six cakes of ice. My job was to make sure each cake was accounted for and to have the truckers sign for everything. We had a contract to produce twenty-five hundred cakes a day and no more, and that's exactly what we shipped each day, at least on paper.

By the time I was released from work, I went home to eat and warm up, then went off to night school. I made only two dollars a day at the ice plant, taking only fourteen dollars a week to my mother who had four mouths to feed. I had to find other ways to make money.

At the ice plant, we were contracted to make twenty-five hundred cakes a day, but we often cheated a bit and made more, which we sold to individual icemen who came by with their trucks. The large ice cakes were solid, but every day the box men loading the ice would accidentally break several cakes, and I would have to get rid of them. We sold those broken pieces directly to homes. I came up with another idea for those broken cakes of ice and a way to solve my money problems.

One of our contracts was with the Borden's Company. They had a big plant two blocks away from us and picked up a load or two of ice every day which they broke up with their choppers and used to keep their milk containers cold during shipping. I started saving the broken pieces of ice for Borden's.

A Dutchman named Heine, a large, bow-legged man with straggly blond hair, hitched up his four-horse team to a big wagon (just like the Anheiser/Bush Budweiser wagons with a double team of Clydesdales) and drove it two city blocks to load up the ice for Borden's. Each day, after he loaded up the solid cakes, Heine asked, "How many cakes you have broke?"

I'd say, "Oh, about six." He told me to put them on the wagon because he could use them anyway. Since they were in pieces, he couldn't tell if I had six cakes or four, and I always told him a little more than it really was.

So, now I was ahead two cakes of ice--me, Nat Serota--and I sold them in pieces to the individual icemen. Borden's was billed through the accounting department (for a little more than they'd actually received), and the icemen paid me cash which I put in my pocket. The number of cakes of ice produced were accounted for and I picked up an extra couple of bucks a day this way. Instead of making fourteen dollars a week, I now made double that. Making ends meet was something you had to engineer in those days.

Heine was a good guy and he often brought me a quart of heavy cream which I'd give to my mother to make ice cream with. You put the cream in a double boiler, add milk, vanilla or chocolate, then put the mixture into an ice cream freezer and churn it. The first time my mother tried to make ice cream, we put the chips of ice and the cream into the freezer, and I churned it and churned it until I thought my arm would come off, but it didn't harden. That was when we got out the recipe book and learned we had to add salt for it to harden. After that, my mother made wonderful ice cream, and we enjoyed it often.

The Knickerbockers Ice Company that my uncles owned was run by the American Ice Company. (New York City is known as a "Knickerbocker's city," thus, the New York Knicks basketball team.) Since this was before the days of refrigeration, when everyone used ice boxes to keep food cold, ice was an important part of the economy. The other major ice company in town, Rubel Ice Company, was privately owned.

It cost eleven cents to make a block of ice. Rubel and Knickerbockers got together and set a price to make sure nobody undercut them. My uncles got fifty-five cents for every cake that went out, and they even made money on top of that. Their contract to produce ice was only for eight months of the year because ice wasn't needed much in New York in the winter months. They made a million dollars a year freezing water!

All good things come to an end, and there came a time when Rubel and Knickerbockers had trouble getting rid of their ice. Refrigerators had started to become popular. So, the Serotas closed down their ice plant and concentrated on their other still-thriving business: the coal yard.

I went to work at the coal yard. After a short time, I decided I wanted a better job there with more responsibility, like I'd had at the ice plant. I wanted to become a "weigh master," the person who weighed the trucks coming in and out, first empty, then loaded with coal. But a weigh master had to be at least eighteen years old and properly licensed. I was only seventeen and that might have presented a problem. Not for me. I always found a way.

I had a cousin, also named Nathan Serota, who was twenty years old. I called the Bureau of Records and told them my name was Nathan Serota and I had lost my birth certificate and needed another copy. I gave them my cousin's birth date, and they sent me a copy of his birth certificate. I then went to the Bureau of Weights and Measures in New York and told them I was Nathan Serota, which I was, and showed them my cousin's birth certificate as proof of my age. I easily passed the test for obtaining a weigh master's license and they issued me the license, simple as that.

I was now a weigh master at my uncles' coal yard. The yard sold coal wholesale by the ton to retailers who resold it and delivered it to homes for use in furnaces. Trucks pulled up on one of two scales, one scale for going in and one for going out, but depending on traffic, you could use them both ways. When the empty truck came in and stopped on the scale I marked down the weight. I sat inside a closed room with a large glass window, looking out at the name of the truck and greeting the driver over a microphone.

I'd ask, "What are you going for?"

The driver might reply that he wanted eight tons of Egg coal (the highest priced coal at about $10 a ton) and perhaps two tons of Nut coal ($7 a ton) or Buckwheat coal (even smaller at $4 a ton).

"Okay, go ahead and load up," I'd tell him.

There were stacks and stacks of coal in the plant which was built above so the trucks drove underneath it to load. After loading, the trucks drove back onto the scales (the only way they could leave), and I weighed them out. If the truck weighed ten tons coming in and twenty tons going out, I charged them for ten tons of coal. Coal was regulated by law and had to be purchased by the ton, or half-ton exactly, no odd amounts. This was so the retailers couldn't screw their customers when they delivered it. It was my job to see it was measured accurately. There were inspectors from the Bureau of Weights and Measures, which they still have today.

After I'd obtained my license illegally and worked as a weigh master for about two weeks, one of my uncles came to me and said, "Nat, we have a problem at our coal yard on the Gowanas Canal. We're missing five thousand tons of coal at the gates of Missouri, don't know who is stealing it and can't understand how. We're going to send you down to work as a weigh master at our plant on the Gowanas Canal."

This canal is in Brooklyn (still there today), and there were lots of boats, oil tankers, and barges going up and down the water past the coal yard. Frank Tuckman, a very big guy about six foot two and in his mid-thirties, was the head weigh master there. His family was in the catering business supplying all the temples and churches, so everybody knew Frank Tuckman. I was sent to work under him, supposedly to help him. I was only there a week, and I discovered where all the coal was going.

The neighborhoods in the area were full of immigrants living in five- or six-story buildings. Most of the apartments had no heating units, just potbelly stoves. Kerosene was the number one oil because they used it both to light the coal in the potbelly stove and to cook with. At that time, the peddlers who sold kerosene were called ice peddlers because they supplied ice, kerosene, and coal, all on the same truck. On their delivery trucks, the kerosene was kept in a metal tank; the ice was kept cool in an ice box on the edge, being sold by the piece; and the coal was stored in pockets in hundred-pound burlap sacks. The men, mostly big, strong Italians, would heft these hundred-pound sacks of coal on their shoulders and walk them up the flights of stairs. Coal cost six dollars a ton at the coal yard (a ton being two thousand pounds). These men didn't know that, and they were being charged way too much for the hundred-pound sacks.

I caught onto the scheme one day when Frank Tuckman went out to lunch and left me as weigh master in charge. Tony Pasqualli came looking for Frank, yelling, "Where's that stinkin' sonoffabitch? He killed me! Said he charged me for twenty-six hundred pounds and I only got twenty-four." In other words, Tuckman had given the Italian an invoice on which he'd made an error on the weight. He didn't do it deliberately, because if he had, they all would have come running back to him like Pasqualli had, but that mistake tipped me off to just what he was doing.

I checked closer and discovered that when Tuckman made the ticket out, the white ticket which was kept for the plant records, he'd put down a thousand pounds of coal (which would satisfy the inspectors), but the peddler actually paid for and received sixteen hundred pounds. Tuckman would leave the correct dollar figure off the top of the invoice, then write it in pencil on the copy he kept. At the end of his shift, he'd cash out and turn the money into the bookkeepers minus the amounts noted in pencil which he'd put directly into his own pocket.

I checked out this theory for two or three days and caught him at it. Then I called the boss and reported Tuckman's scam and the amount of money he'd stolen. I was immediately promoted to head weigh master--an awesome responsibility for a seventeen-year-old--which I held for three more years.

Johnny Delphino was the driver of a coal truck, working with another man to deliver coal. On the truck, they had a shoot and a big wooden barrel which they filled with coal. They rolled the barrel to the house and emptied the coal into another shoot there. Johnny was an Italian, mid-thirties, stocky, and not terribly tall, but he was a special man, and popular.

Many times during the day, Fay, my girlfriend who worked at the coal yard, answered the phone and took orders from women who asked that their coal be delivered by Johnny Delphino specifically. This was Brooklyn, and word got around; everyone knew Delphino was endowed, that it came to his knees. Women ordered coal deliveries after their husbands had left for work, and Johnny "the lover" was busy every day with the ladies while his helper unloaded coal into their houses.

The business grew. By the following year, my uncles had acquired more land right on the corner of the canal and began building a big oil terminal there. (Fifty years later it still stands in the same spot.) When the new plant was built, I was promoted again, this time to running it. It was a huge plant which sold fuel oil, number two oil (which people still buy today for heating purposes), kerosene, and number six oil used for heating big apartment houses. I not only had to operate it, I had to order huge quantities of the oil at maybe a quarter of a million gallons one day to two million gallons the next, depending on the demand. We had several suppliers, such as Esso and Petro Petroleum, and I was constantly fighting with them for the best price. In addition to running the plant, I personally sold four million gallons of oil and kerosene per year wholesale.

During the day, I ran the plant and sold oil to various contractors in the office, then at night I had to meet the damned ship coming in to deliver at all hours. And I had to learn how to measure oil because oil is delivered at a certain temperature. The hotter the oil is, the more it expands, so the companies try to warm it up when they ship it in the tankers. You get screwed when it shrinks again. If a tanker came in at two o'clock in the morning, Nat had to be there to measure the God-damned oil.

One day, I had a fight with the boss. His son, my cousin, Norman, had graduated from Cornell a week before, and my uncle asked me to teach him to run the business, teach him everything I knew. I jumped to what, in retrospect, was a wrong conclusion. I thought I was being asked to train my replacement and assumed I'd be out of a job. "How can we both work here?" I demanded angrily. "What's going to happen to me when your son takes over your business?" My uncle tried to assure me I'd still have my job, but I didn't believe him and refused to train Norman. We had a big fight about it, and I quit.

This being 1942, the war had started. Now, here I was, twenty-two years old, looking for a job. I was supporting my family: a brother, two sisters, and my mother. I still lived at home and was used to a good salary. At the oil plant, I'd been making thirty-five dollars a week, which was a half salary for running the place, but they had also bought me a brand new 1941 club-coupe Oldsmobile worth $823. It was a gorgeous car--right out of the show room. That alone should tell you what kind of money I was making and how I was living.

But I always found a way to land on my feet. Three days later, I saw an ad in the New York Times for employees to work at the Pennsylvania Railroad.

8

Finances on Track at the Pennsylvania Railroad

The war was on, and soldiers were being shipped all over the country by train. The railroad was busy and short of help, so they were glad to see me. At that time, Pennsylvania Railroad was the biggest railroad in the northeast. They owned Penn Station in New York, which was much nicer than Grand Central Station. Penn Station was large and ran from 31st Street to 33rd Street and took up a whole avenue from 7th Avenue to 8th Avenue.

I got a job, at first with the information bureau upstairs on the third floor of Penn Station, giving out information about the trains, such as what time they departed or arrived and when and where they stopped. I got paid well--$189 dollars per month. It was more money than I'd made at the oil plant, and I was on my own. I didn't have to put up with my uncles.

But, after only three days, the job drove me nuts. All I was doing was sitting around answering the phone, and that definitely wasn't enough for me. I approached the boss, Mr. John Horsch, who ran the ticket office and the information bureau. Penn Station had over two hundred and sixty ticket sellers in the rotunda. That's where I wanted to work, where the action was.   I told Mr. Horsch how much I appreciated the job he'd given me, but I simply couldn't stay up there on that dull information counter. He asked me what kind of job I wanted, and I replied that I wanted to sell tickets because I'd make more money and get to see the public.

Mr. Horsch, a small, elderly gentlemen who always wore a hat, laughed. "Hey, kid, you don't know how to sell tickets. You got to learn to sell tickets. We sell tickets here for the whole country, for every railroad. They're called Interline tickets. Those booths over there . . ." he gestured with a sweeping hand, " . . . those booths sell local tickets on the Pennsylvania Railroad to Washington, and downstairs, they sell tickets on the Long Island Railroad. You want to go downstairs?"

"No," I answered. "I don't want to go to the Long Island Railroad. I want to do something more important."

He nodded, his expression as serious as mine, but the hint of a smile played around his lips. I was twenty-two years old and ready to take on the world. "Well," he said, "Here you get paid two hundred and twenty-nine dollars a month, but you have to learn how to sell tickets first. Tell you what I'm going to do with you, kid. I'll ask one of the men to teach you, but you got to learn on your own time. You keep working upstairs at your current salary, then when you get through, you come down here and learn to sell tickets without pay. If you're that keen on changing jobs, we'll see."

Now, Mr. Horsch . . . he is a man I will never forget. He was in his sixties with a married son and several grandchildren. When his son died, he married his daughter-in-law and raised his son's family. And he had faith in me, a young kid with potential. He allowed me an opportunity.

That afternoon, Mr. Horsch introduced me to an Irishman, Bill Boye, a lovely guy who, at that time, was about fifty years old. Bill belonged to the union, which meant he couldn't be fired and would eventually receive a good pension. A big, good-natured guy, he'd been with the railroad a long time and was highly respected by everyone there.

"Hey, Bill, this kid thinks he can sell tickets," said Mr. Horsch. "I told him he's got to learn to sell tickets before we can give him a job down here. See what you can teach him."

After three days with Bill, I told Mr. Horsch I knew how to sell tickets, and Bill agreed that I did. The boss couldn't believe I'd learned how to sell tickets all over the country in just three days, but I showed him what I knew and told him I could start the next day. Bill assured him that if I ran into trouble he would help me. What could Mr. Horsch do but agree to let me start the following morning? Although only twenty-two, I was almost bald and looked older than I was. They put down that I was twenty-nine when I got the job.

Everything was done by seniority in the railroad office. You bid on your job; if you wanted to change hours, days, or even to a particular window, you had to bid on it. The bidder with the most seniority got the job. I got a break--instead of working nights I was now working days. I'd figured out the system and decided I was better off taking an irregular job each day rather than a permanent window because I could make $229 a month and work days. An irregular job meant selling Interline tickets at any time during the day to cover any available position. The other ticket sellers were accommodating and helped me when I needed it. Within a very short time I became the best ticket seller Pennsylvania Railroad had.

At that time, the railroad only had three Jews working for them. We were discriminated against then. There was always a relationship between gentiles and Jews in large companies, and Jews were not often hired. There were two big hotels in Hershey, Pennsylvania (where the Hershey Chocolate company was located), and years ago, no Jews were allowed there. At Penn Station they didn't know I was Jewish. They called me Nate.

First, I learned how to sell tickets, then I learned how to make real money. Throughout my life I always found a way to make that *extra* dollar. I believe there exists in every business a legitimate, legal way to *make more money*. Let me tell you something that I often told my sons: Anybody with a brain in their head, whether working for someone else or in business for themselves, can make an extra dollar. Seriously, in various ways--and I don't mean stealing--you can always come up with an add-on, a new idea, to make that extra buck.

At the Pennsylvania Railroad there were special tickets for the sleeper cars and Pullman cars. Pullman tickets were first class and cost two and a half times more than coach tickets and interline tickets; they were the most expensive in the country. At first, every now and then, a young man without an advance ticket would come up to my window and request a roomette on a sleeper for that very night. Often it would be a foggy, rainy night, and I'd tell him I wasn't sure I could get it, but I'd call reservations to find out. There would be no roomettes available, no space. The customer would then tell me that if I could somehow find the space he'd take care of me. He'd give me a tip for helping him out. From then on I got wise.

In my experience with the railroad, I regularly received an extra five dollars or an extra ten as a tip for finding people space. Once, I even got a $1,000 tip (a staggering amount then) for getting *an entire car* for Mr. Bonomo of Bonomo Turkish Taffy, the biggest taffy maker in the country and the sponsor of Milton Berle's first T.V. program. From that night on, Victor Bonomo and I became friends. Whenever he needed space on a train, he always called Serota.

The first night I met Mr. Bonomo at the station, he wanted a whole car on the Florida Special to Miami Beach in the middle of March! Even *I* figured *that* was impossible. But nonetheless, I told Bonomo I'd see what I could do for him. I went to Fred Loeffel, the head man in charge of everything at the Penn Station rotunda, and brazenly asked him to give me an entire car on the fanciest all-Pullman train they had going to Florida, during the busy tourist season.

Loeffel shook his head and laughed. "Serota, you've got to be kidding."

I proceeded to explain just who Victor Bonomo was and just how much taffy he regularly shipped on the Pennsylvania Railroad. I told him Bonomo was a personal friend of mine who'd asked me to get the car for him and reminded him again of the great amount of revenue the man's company provided for the railroad.

Loeffel slanted me a look from the corner of his eye as if dubiously weighing my argument. He knew I had a reputation as a deal-maker who'd sold hot space to customers in the past, and he didn't want to help me put more cash in my pocket. Dismissing me abruptly, he said, "I'll let you know."

Four days later, I found a note in my box from Loeffel. I got the whole car on the Florida Special for the date I'd requested, and Victor Bonomo handed me $1,000 cash as a gratuity for getting it!

I always had the drive to make money, the hunger for it. My clients were the biggest companies in the country because I was the smartest, wittiest ticket seller there. Many of my regular customers were famous people, such as Admiral Hyman Rickover, Eleanor Roosevelt, Colonel Charles Lindbergh, Jock Whitney, and W.R. Hearst.

9

The Army

Unbeknownst to me, Uncle Leon had written a letter to the draft board after I quit the job at the oil plant, *because* I had quit, so I was drafted into the Army in 1942. I'd been a successful ticket seller for less than a year then, but in those days, the union protected your job when you were called into the Service; it was the law. When you got out, you returned to your same job.

I spent thirty-seven long months in the Army. The only good thing about my stint in the Army was my discharge. What they say about the Army teaching a boy to be a man is nothing but bullshit. A young man should be hired by the Army and paid well because it is one hell of a rough time, no matter what it's promoted to be. The Army, in my opinion, is not a good deal.

I started out as a buck-ass private and wound up First Sergeant Nat Serota in less than two years. Despite my dislike of the situation I was in, I succeeded in the Army and became the kingpin of my Antiaircraft Battery. As First Sergeant, I was the top man in the unit without actually becoming an officer. How did I become first sergeant, you ask? By being me and being smart. I pulled more crap in the Army than at any other time in my life.

I was young, ambitious, eager to grow, and driven to get promotions. Basically, I screwed the officers into thinking I was smarter than they were. I handled reports in the office, payroll and such. Full of youthful vim and vinegar, I always followed through and went the extra mile or found another angle. I made things happen by being in the office at the right time and by being smart enough to see opportunities and seize them.

When I was drafted, I went from Long Island to Camp Stewart, near Savannah, Georgia. There I was assigned to an antiaircraft outfit--Battery 842AAA. From day one until I got out of the Army, I stayed in the same company, and that was very rare. It presented me with opportunities to get to know people well. When I arrived at Camp Stewart, I met the young officers who had just come out of officer training at Candidate School. I quickly realized those officers didn't know their asses from a hole in the ground.

Guns were delivered to the base all crated up. We opened up the crates which contained 40-mm antiaircraft guns--those canons on wheels that you use to shoot down an airborne enemy from a plane. Nobody knew what the hell they were doing with these guns.

At that moment, it hit me squarely that a person could get killed in the Army from incompetence alone, without even getting to the front line. I didn't go into the Army to get killed, so I pulled a fast one.

Prior to my stint, I had worked in the oil business about a year before the war started. One day, I'd stepped out of my car in Brooklyn near the oil terminal and an AWVS lady driving a station wagon, a wooden vehicle, hit me and physically knocked me over. My ankle wound up underneath her wheel. I was in the hospital for a week with broken ligaments in my ankle, and for some time afterwards, although healed, my ankle would swell up on me. When I was nineteen and twenty, I'd use the swelling to get away with things.

Now, I found myself in the Army, and I wanted to get the hell out before I got killed. I didn't think anyone in the Army knew what they were doing, and that seriously worried me. By the end of the day, when my ankle normally swelled, I went to the doctor and showed him. I pretended I couldn't walk or run because my foot was killing me, and I used the swelling to hit the sick book every day. I desperately wanted out of the Army.

Captain Luntz, my commanding officer, was a big, husky guy with jowls and a chubby, red face who spoke with a southern accent. Everyone else had to march eight or ten miles a day, but I always goofed off because of my bad foot. I made out I was sick and couldn't run or march so I'd be given an office job. But Captain Luntz, that son-of-a-bitch, figured out I was lying and f-----g around, so he made things tougher on me. He knew the score, picked on me and blocked my attempts to get an early discharge. His efforts failed, and I wound up being promoted instead.

Oddly, First Sergeant Walker worked in the battery office without knowing how to write a report or type. I helped him out and wrote the reports for him. Sergeant Walker pushed for me to become a private first class so I could work with him all the time. Captain Luntz didn't want me to get off that easily, but at last he okayed Walker's request for help. So began my career in the office of the battery unit.

Through working in the office, I became a PFC and made it as far as corporal. The colonel of Battery Headquarters came to know me and noticed I did a good job. He said he wanted to transfer me to his office at headquarters and promote me to sergeant. He called Captain Luntz and told him he wanted to "get this kid, Serota, up to headquarters." The captain refused to allow it. I was in the office and knew the colonel was going to call, so I made sure I overheard the conversation. Luntz went on and on about how I was needed there to help Walker. Well, I knew Luntz just didn't like me and was trying to screw up my career. However, the colonel was *the boss*, and he found a way to transfer me anyway. I went to Headquarters Battery, and that was how I became First Sergeant.

During the time I was at Camp Stewart, Georgia, our battery was shipped to New York where there were about ten batteries. Each battery had five divisions: A, B, C, and D Battery, and Headquarters Battery. From New York, thousands of men were being shipped to Germany. Everyone in the batteries was sent off to Germany and fought in the famous Battle of the Bulge where most of them were killed. Inexplicably, two batteries were shipped back to Camp Stewart!

A couple of months after my battery had returned to Camp Stewart, we were shipped to Seattle, Washington, and from there to the Pacific. Sadly, my mother died while I was in Seattle, and I received a call there with the news. She died suddenly of a heart attack. I got leave to fly home for a few days and attend her funeral, then I had to return to the Army and go immediately overseas. It was a tough time for me. I recall suffering and being mentally disturbed and thinking of the hard times.

Although grateful not to be killed in the Army, I felt I was wasting my time there, and I was anxious to get on with my life. We were originally shipped to Oahu, Hawaii, where the battleships were bombed at Pearl Harbor. Every few months they'd ship us from Pearl Harbor to different areas and out to other islands. In the fourteen months I was overseas I didn't see any action and felt like I was just visiting Hawaii.

I was terribly seasick from the moment the ship pulled out of the harbor in Seattle, for the whole nine days of the voyage to Hawaii. We were with the last group of ships that were bombed by the Japanese crossing the Pacific. I was aboard the steamship *Johnson*. The Japanese sank the tail boat at the end of our convoy: *The President Jackson*. Leaning over the rail with the rolling seas under me, dizzy with sickness, I wished they'd sink us too. My head not being balanced to the movement of the waves was what caused my sickness, and once I walked on *terra-firma* everything was great.

We arrived in Hawaii on Thanksgiving Day in 1943 and spent it at Kahuku Hills which was owned by Princess Kamahamaha, whose father was the famous King Kamahamaha. They owned the camp where we were stationed in tents. To celebrate Thanksgiving we were served turkey with all the trimmings--quite a spread.

I remember the bugs and heat in Hawaii were something terrible. Pineapples grew in the fields right outside our tents. (It takes eighteen months for a pineapple to grow, and that's what makes them so expensive.) There were signs in the fields warning people not to eat the pineapple, threatening a five hundred dollar fine and a year in jail. Naturally, Serota and a half dozen guys *simply had to* take barracks bags out to the fields and load them up with pineapples. But if you eat too many pineapples, you get diarrhea so badly you want to die. The next day a bunch of us went to the hospital, half dead from eating so many pineapples. I couldn't eat pineapple for about five years after that.

When we Caucasian Americans first arrived in Hawaii where most of the local girls were Asian, we thought they were ugly--no breasts and skinny as rails. We used to talk about them, but we were young soldiers looking for girls, and after three or four weeks, we decided they looked pretty good after all. Today, when a friend of mine goes to Hawaii, I ask them to look up my family in Oahu. I laugh at their puzzled faces and jokingly tell them I was there for fourteen months in the Army and raised a whole family.

Perhaps being in the Service is better today, but it wasn't good in my time. It wasn't a positive place for anyone to "get an education and become a man." The people who benefitted most from the Army were mainly boys who lived in poor areas without the opportunity to get a good job. If they were smart and worked hard in the Army, they could grow and gain experience and obtain the basic education they had been denied at home.

For me, my business career had been well underway when it was interrupted by the Army. In my view, the Army should be a profession, a personal choice.

10

First Furlough, Getting Married

The Army was selling bonds while I was a hotshot in the office with Walker. All the soldiers were encouraged to buy U.S. savings bonds to help keep the Army going. Of course, that was all political bullshit, but I bought a bond because they gave you a three-day pass as incentive. Now, I certainly didn't want to spend my precious three-day pass in Georgia. One of my buddies was the camp cook, Guzzie, another guy from Brooklyn. Guzzie also bought a bond and got a three-day pass.

I wanted to go to see my girlfriend, Fay, and goof off for the weekend, so I suggested we grab the fast train to New York, the Champion. "I have my Pennsylvania Railroad pass which is good on the Atlantic Coast Line," I explained to Guzzie. "Come with me and we'll both get to New York."

"How will you get me on the train?" asked Guzzie

"Don't worry about it. I'm in the office. I'll make up a phony emergency pass." I stole the correct form and typed up an emergency which stated that someone in his family had died, then signed our captain's name it.

It was not unusual to take off early, especially if you had a furlough. The day I planned to leave, I told Lieutenant Hughes, a nice looking guy with light brown hair, that I wanted to escape early in order to catch the Champion to New York. "I'm going to screw off till three or four o'clock before midnight breaks," I said.

When he asked how I was going to get on the train, I explained I had worked for the railroad and still had my pass. He raised his hand in a wave, "I didn't see nothing. You take off and I'll work for ya."

I took off with Guzzie, and we hitched a ride to Savannah. We were in a hurry to get to the station well ahead of the train so we could walk into the railroad office and show the emergency pass. The guy who stopped to give us a lift asked us where we were going, then said it would cost us ten bucks each for the forty-minute ride. We were in no position to argue, so we gave him the money and accepted the ride to Savannah.

I rushed back home to see my girlfriend and, at the spur of the moment on my first furlough from the Army, we decided to elope. In those days in the state of New York, you had to get blood tests taken, then wait two or three days for the results before you could get married. I was on a short furlough, and we didn't have that kind of time. I called my sister, Betty, in Baltimore, the only member of my family who knew about Fay and I, and told her we wanted to speak to her Rabbi right away. We hopped on a train for Baltimore, then Betty took us directly to the temple where we met with the Rabbi in his quarters. He married Fay and I immediately, and we spent our wedding night at a nice hotel in Baltimore.

After three days of marriage and madness, I had to return to Camp Stewart, but the Champion didn't leave until the following morning. I was a corporal then and reported for duty at six o'clock in the morning. Guzzie had returned the previous day to make sure he'd be on time. My train didn't even arrive in Savannah until eight. It was now eleven o'clock. I'd taken a bus from the train station in Savannah to a small town outside the base, then walked in from there.

At the time, I had a helper working under me, a Polish kid named

Jaswack, who had a bad heart and didn't belong in the Army. When I walked into the office he said in a hushed voice, "Serota, you're in trouble. They traced you. Captain Luntz found out from Lieutenant Hughes that you left early to catch the train, and now you're back late. They're going to put you on court martial."

Just then, Luntz entered the office and barked, "Serota, I want to see you in my office."

I followed the captain to his office. I had to think fast. Luntz eyed me with a stern glare and asked where I had been at six o'clock that morning.

I said calmly, "The train was late and I got stuck on it. I went home."

"I was going to report you AWOL, charge you, and put you in jail for a while, but I've changed my mind," he said gruffly. "Walker says he needs you. No passes for two months, Serota. Dismissed."

I worked in the office, so I signed my own passes for the next two months and had one every weekend. Two years later, after I got out of the Army and returned to work at the railroad, a man came up to my ticket booth and asked for a ticket to Atlanta, Georgia. It was none other than Luntz! He was as surprised to see me working there as I was to see him. We talked briefly, and he told me he'd married a girl from the Bronx.

Now, here's the payoff. At the Army camp in Battery A, I thought there had only been three Jews, myself and two others. However, one day I had been working in the office and spotted Luntz's dog tags on top of the desk, so I looked at them. Whatever your nationality, it was printed on your dog tags and his had a "J" for Jewish. That explained a few things. Luntz had picked on me and another Jewish guy named Broidy because he didn't want the other officers to think that he was treating us special and favoring Jews. He gave us a bigger shaft than anyone else. I brought that up when I met him at the railroad and he told me about his marriage.

"You son-of-a-bitch, the girl you married from the Bronx, is she Jewish too?"

45

"Yeah," he said.

"You picked on us. You picked on Broidy," I accused him. In a way, I made my peace with Luntz that day when I sold him a train ticket. We actually ended up laughing together about our shared Army experience.

11

Fay

In 1943, at the age of twenty-two, I had married Fay. We'd met almost two years earlier when she worked as a bookkeeper and receptionist on the switchboard at the same coal yard where I had been head weigh master. There were probably five or six girls working there, but I was attracted to Fay. Since I didn't have a car then, I used to get a lift from the boss in order to catch the trolley car going to Coney Island Avenue and Avenue "J" in Brooklyn. Fay rode with us every day, and my boss dropped her off first on Cortleyou Road. During the rides, I grew to like her, and vice versa. When he dropped me off, I'd walk back to meet Fay secretly.

She was ten years older than I, and in those days, an older woman with a younger man was somewhat of a scandal. Fay was my first true love (aside from Peggy O'Malley at fifteen), and no one knew I was seeing her every Saturday night. At this time, young men and women didn't drink alcohol, so we'd have a bite to eat or go to the movies and see romantic stories with Clark Gable in them. I didn't have a car then, but I borrowed one every chance I could and drove the twenty minutes to her home in Boro-Park from where I lived in Midwood, Brooklyn.

One night, I borrowed a car from an acquaintance, dropped my mother off at the movies in Midwood and drove to pick up Fay. My mother had a bad heart, and I had arranged to pick her up at 10:30 and take her home on my way back. Meanwhile, Fay and I parked at Coney Island Park near her house. Fay was about to leave for a two-week vacation in the mountains, and I wanted to give her a proper send off. It was a balmy spring evening and lots of people strolled by or sat on their front porches. Suddenly, two men yanked open the rear door and climbed into the car. There was a gun pressed hard to the back of my head.

At that time, I earned about thirty-five dollars a week, and Fay made about twenty. The two men stole all my money plus everything out of her bag and the ring she was wearing. They told me to start the car and, with the gun still pressed to my head, had me drive about six blocks. The peculiar thing I remember about the experience is that, even though we were in the middle of being held up at gun point, neither of us were hysterical. A surprising calm had come over me.

I tried to reason with the men, saying, "please, this lady is going on vacation tomorrow." When they instructed us to get out of the car, I explained it wasn't my car and asked them what they were going to do with it. Anyone can appreciate the embarrassment of borrowing a friend's car only to have it stolen out from under you. However, I think the robbers were drunk or on drugs, not at all sympathetic to my feelings. We got out of the car, an Oldsmobile, and they peeled away in it, burning rubber. Three days later, the police found the car. I don't remember how my mother got home that night. The incident made me angry, rather than scared. That was the first time I had been held up, but it would not be the last.

My secret romance with Fay was eventually uncovered. Somehow my older sister found out about Fay and told my mother. They were upset that I was going with a woman who was ten years older than me. To pacify my mother, I claimed I had stopped seeing Fay. Instead, I just disappeared on the weekends, and my family didn't know where the hell I was. I worked night and day in those days (as I always have), so they assumed I was working.

I was with Fay. We were never gone overnight--you didn't do that then--but for a year we spent all our days off together. After I left the coal yard and went to sell tickets at the railroad we didn't see each other every day like we had while working together. She was still my girl when I started at the railroad, and still my girl eight months later when I got drafted. That was why, on my first furlough, we eloped. My mother went crazy when we told her we were married, but eventually Fay and my mother really learned to care for each other.

After our hurried wedding in Baltimore, I had to return to the Service because there was a war on. Every day while I was away, I wrote my mother a letter, and I wrote another one to Fay. One time I wrote Fay confessing I'd lost my money playing craps and asking her to please send me some more. I wrote my mother at the same time, naturally not telling her I'd lost my money, but I accidentally put Fay's letter into my mother's envelope.

My mother called Fay to tell her she'd read the wrong letter. "That phony son-of-a-bitch, he was playing cards and shooting craps. He's sent you a letter asking for money. Don't you send him a nickel," insisted my mother.

Of course, Fay sent me the money.

I was in the Army for two and a half years, and during that time, Fay lived in a three-bedroom apartment with her mother, brother and sister. Her father had died just ten days after we were married. Fay made her own living working at different jobs since she didn't get any money from me--I didn't make any in the Army. When I was discharged, I went back to work at the railroad. I moved in with Fay's family until we could find an apartment of our own. So many people had been released from the military at that time that apartments were very difficult to find.

12

Making Money as Number A59

When I was discharged from the Army, I went back to my ticket booth in the rotunda at Penn Station, all the more eager to make big bucks. As well as the tickets, I sold insurance at twenty-five cents a day for up to five thousand dollars coverage. Now, talk about an angle . . . . There were two hundred men working there, some for forty years, and the idiots had not caught on to how to do this. They were happy simply collecting their $229 a month and going home to their wives every night. I discovered that for every twenty-five cents worth of insurance I sold, I'd get a nickel--twenty percent of every insurance dollar I sold! I fast became the biggest insurance salesman they had in the whole country. I received an extra four to five hundred dollars a month in commission for selling insurance, as well as extra tips for finding available space for people, making more on commission and tips than I did on my salary.

It is interesting how I got all that available space. I found out when the seating diagrams for the different cars on the trains came out. It makes me smile today when I think about it, because I was so young then. I made a lot of money and a lot of love. I had many girlfriends in the office, and those girlfriends gave me the information I needed to book the space I would later sell. I would make an extra fifty to a hundred dollars a day in tips when it became known that Serota had the space. I had a lot of fun in those days.

I pulled yet another fast one. During the busy winter season, the Atlantic Coast Line ran the popular, all-coach Champion and The Florida Special, a deluxe all-Pullman train regularly from New York to Miami. The Seaboard Line operated The Silver Meteor which carried coach and Pullman cars. All the trains going to Florida at this time of year were packed full. There simply was no space to be had on any of them. But Nat Serota had space.

When the diagrams came out, I told the girls I was seducing what space I wanted. Even if I didn't actually have the space *sold* I'd take it, because I knew I'd easily be able to sell it. I speculated, investing my own money in space on the trains by buying most of it up. I had a stack of tickets on that highly sought-after Florida Special with an elastic band around it bulging in my pocket every day. The whole God-damned season I had space no one else had access to.

If I couldn't get all the space I needed from the girls upstairs in the local office, I called my sister, Betty, in Baltimore. Each train had a certain amount of space allotted to the ticket sellers in Baltimore, Washington, and Philadelphia on their diagrams. Betty would make reservations for me, then take the train on my employee pass and buy up tickets in those other cities. I then cashed in her tickets and reissued them out of New York. Legally, I could change the space and put the customer on at New York instead of Baltimore. I worked all the angles and did stuff you couldn't imagine.

Young and hungry, I worked all evening and into the night, maybe until one or two o'clock in the morning if someone didn't show up at midnight. I started working straight through two periods with overtime pay. The railroad was glad to put me to work because they needed help.

One time, we had a Pullman car arriving in Philadelphia for the Army-Navy parade and big football game there. Another ticket seller wasn't able to show up, so I was called in at time-and-a-half for overtime. We started off each shift with a hundred dollars in silver and small bills in our banks, so as usual, that morning I went inside to get my bank and my number stamp. The stamper had a large base with a big rubber thing on the top and the number of the ticket seller on a bronze plate. My number was A59.

Everybody was running to the parlor car for anything first class going to Philadelphia the day of the Army-Navy game, and I walked across the busy floor with my bank and number stamp, all set for a brisk day of making money. Suddenly, Mr. Loeffel, the head man of the whole railroad, approached, wiggling his finger at me. "Serota," he said in a serious tone, "I want to see you."

"Oh, good morning, Mr. Loeffel." I wondered why he'd stopped me on such a busy day. "Sure, but this is my third shift, and I must get to the parlor car right now."

"I know, but I want to ask you a question. I've been watching you, Serota, and I think you're wrapping up the insurance."

"What do you mean? You've been watching me? But I'm here mostly at night."

"I've been watching your tours." He eyed me quizzically. "You're the only one in the history of the railroad who has ever made so much money in insurance commissions."

Oh no, I thought. Was he accusing me of screwing the customers? I knew it was true; that was what I'd done by selling the customers insurance they thought cost a total of twenty-five cents without explaining they were actually paying twenty-five cents *for each day* they were away. I responded without hesitation. "Sir, did you ever check my tours and how many tickets I sell? I sell more tickets than anyone in this whole railroad."

"Yeah, I checked, and you're right, you do. But you're a wise guy and I still think you're wrapping up the insurance. If I catch you, you're out, and don't think I won't put you on trial."

"Have you ever had a complaint about me, Sir?" I asked innocently.

"No, kid," he admitted, "but if I ever do . . . . Now, get back to work. It's busy."

"Yes, Sir." I nodded soberly, then set up my window and started to sell tickets like gangbusters. I had enough guts to keep up everything I was doing, and they never fired me.

When you work for the railroad you belong to the union, and they can't fire you unless they put you on trial for doing something wrong. You *never* stole from the railroad, and if you made honest mistakes, you paid for them out of your own pocket. At the end of your shift, all the money went to the accounting department and it had to balance with the tickets you sold. If not, it came out of your pay. If it was a really large amount, they would sometimes let us take it out over two or three months, but we paid for our mistakes. And I made my share.

For instance, when my son, Charles, was born I was extremely elated. I had to work that night, and I remember passing out cigars to everybody because I was so proud and excited. That night I made a costly error when I sold a round-trip coach ticket to Kalispell, Montana, a very long way from New York. I only charged for a one-way and had to pay the difference, seventy dollars, out of my own pocket.

13

To All The Girls I've Loved Before

Should I be honest about my love life in this book? Hell, yes. I had a good time with the ladies, especially while I worked at the railroad when I was younger.

"Sure, be honest about it," my wife, Vivian, agreed, *"put the love letters in, too. It was all before you married me. All of it is fun, all the girlfriends you had; you were a devil."*

I wasn't just making money at Penn Station; I was making the girls. Not only did I have beautiful girls in the office to love, I had female customers who were beautiful too. I became acquainted with some of them and had a number of affairs.

At the railroad, I always managed to escape getting caught buying up all that extra space, but I remember having some close calls. One time I made reservations for space in Washington and Baltimore, then had to travel by train, using my pass, to pick up the tickets. On the return trip to New York, with thousands of dollars worth of tickets in my bulging pockets, I ran into Jim Logan, one of the head clerks I worked under, on the same God-damned train.

"Hey, hey," Jim said, "what are you doing here?"

Here I was with rolls of tickets practically spilling out of my pockets. I didn't even blink, and a good cover story came instantly to mind. I told him my sister was sick and lived in Baltimore and I'd been to visit her. He bought that story, but he never thought I was Jewish and didn't believe my name was Nathan.

Jim Logan was tough but nice. One night while I was working, at about 6:30 p.m., it was quiet in the rotunda at Penn Station. Along came a beautiful, young lady--a school teacher with long, brown hair, round, full breasts, and legs that wouldn't quit. She asked for a ticket to Los Angeles for the following day. She told me she'd just come in from New Jersey and planned to stay in the hotel across the street, but she'd left her baggage at the station downtown.

While I tapped out her tickets, my imagination worked overtime thinking of the ways I could help make her night in the hotel one to remember. Too bad I'd just started my shift. With her tickets in my hand, I went back to talk to Jim. "Jim, you want to see a beautiful woman? Come to my window and take a good look."

He followed me back to the window. After staring numbly at her for a moment, he cleared his throat and said in an official sounding voice, "Nate, can I see you back here please."

Once out of earshot, Jim exclaimed, "God, is she a knockout. Did you make her?"

"I didn't even try making her. I just started work at five-thirty."

"If you can make her, take off," Jim said. "What do you care about your shift? I'm the boss. I'll take care of it for you."

What a guy! I went back to my window, gave the beautiful school teacher her tickets for California, and promptly made a date with her. I usually kept my car parked at Penn Station--illegally--by taking care of the cops. That night I told them I was working and needed to take her downtown to get her bags to ship to California. I stayed with Alma at the hotel until three in the morning and never did return to work that night. Jim signed me out at one o'clock, and I got paid for having fun.

Alma was a terrific lady, a riot, really hot stuff. She later wrote me cards from California for months. She'd arrived there without mishap, even though it turned out I'd been so flustered by her beauty that I'd made a mistake on her ticket. I found out the following day when one of my coworkers, Russ, informed me that I'd made out the ticket wrong, and he'd fixed it for her. When he commented on Alma's beauty, I simply had to brag and told him I'd been with her all night. Russ was about sixty years old. He was amazed.

Penn Station is on the corner of 7th and 8th Avenues, and there are two well-known hotels directly across from the station, each on opposite corners--both very elegant and famous landmarks--The Hotel Pennsylvania and the New Yorker. Many times I visited the room of a gorgeous lady in those two hotels, but I never rented a room in either one. Like Alma, most of them had invited me up to their rooms while they were staying to wait for trains.

One afternoon I was making love to a beautiful woman who had taken a room at the Pennsylvania to wait for her husband who had gone out of town. He wasn't supposed to return for quite some time. Right in the middle of the main event the phone rang, and she couldn't ignore it. Lucky for us, she didn't. It was her husband calling from the lobby, asking her to meet him downstairs. She scrambled into her clothes and got the hell out of the room. I never dressed so fast in my life. Later, when she came over to pick up the train tickets she'd ordered from me, she bade me a wistful goodbye and explained that her husband had returned early.

At the railroad ticket booth, all kinds of women crossed my path and caught my youthful attention. Some were well-dressed buyers from department stores who paid me extra gratuities for tough-to-get space on the trains. I'll never forget one beauty from Akron, Ohio. She was in her thirties, small, thin, and very beautiful, also very married. She always asked for a first-class roomette return to Akron whenever she came to New York, and I always found it for her. And when my lovely Akron buyer didn't show up for a few months, I missed her. She finally called to say she was coming to New York and suggested we have dinner. I always had extra money, cash in my pocket, at this time in my life, so I could well afford to take her out to a really nice restaurant. Soft music played in the background, and I drank in the delicate aroma of French cooking mixed with her perfume as she sat at the table across from me.

"You son-of-a-bitch," she said too loudly, then dropped her voice and continued, "The reason I haven't been here in three months is because you got me pregnant. I went to get an abortion and, while I was in the hospital, I cursed the shit out of you."

Two days later, when she went back to Akron, I had her ticket in my drawer which her company would pay for. When she came to my window, I closed up so I could see her off. We were lovers again before she departed. When I finally put her on the train, I discovered I'd lost her ticket; I vividly remember having a small, blue, first-class ticket, but it was gone. I went back and bought another one, paying for it myself.

I had so much fun in my youth, so many wild opportunities. Girls came around all over the place--at work, on the trains, at the ticket counter. I'd even tuck them into bed at night in their roomettes on the trains. One night, I noticed Shirley Sloane standing at the back of my ticket line. I told everyone in line that I was closing immediately, so they had to go to another ticket booth. Some things were more important than making money. I went off to spend the night with Shirley at the New Yorker. I saw her regularly, whenever she passed through the city. After telling her sister she was in love with me and wanted to marry me, she even brought her sister to meet me. I didn't want to marry. And besides, Shirley was already married.

I put a stop to my affair with Shirley Sloane after I met her husband and learned what a nice guy he was. He came to my ticket booth one night when it was snowing heavily and all the planes and trains were booked. A children's clothes manufacturer from Milwaukee, Mr. Sloane was trying to get home from a business trip. Amazingly, Shirley had told him if he was ever in trouble getting a train to look up Nat Serota.

"I'm Mr. Sloane," he said, extending his hand. "My wife, Shirley, told me you could help me get space on the train. I sure hope you can."

"Oh, Shirley Sloane," I said, gulping. "Yes, I think I remember her. What do you need?"

He explained that he wanted a roomette on the express train to Chicago, a very fast train leaving at six p.m. It was snowing and I doubted I could get it, but I offered to try. I told him to come back in half an hour, just before the train departed, and sure enough, I got him a bedroom to Chicago. He was a nice man, and he brought me a five-pound box of the finest candy when he returned to get on the train.

I called Shirley shortly after that and said, "I'll see you as a friend--we can have dinner together--but I'm never taking you to bed again." I did have dinner with Shirley a couple of times when she passed through town, but I never slept with her again.

I have few regrets and remember my wild, youthful days with fondness. However, early on in my career as a ticket seller, a gorgeous blonde in her forties wearing an expensive sable coat came by looking for a roomette to Pittsburgh. It was six o'clock at night, and I assured her I could get her the roomette, not to worry. She was the most magnificent woman I'd ever seen, wearing such fine clothes. I didn't realize she was making eyes at me. I was so young and stupid that I didn't understand she wanted me to come to her room. I would later tell both Fay and Vivian the story about that missed opportunity. To this day, I've always regretted blowing that opportunity.

Even after I left the railroad with its wealth of gorgeous women, opportunities for affairs presented themselves. I was still married to Fay, and in those days, I was gambling regularly. I used to go out every night to pick up a newspaper to see what the horses were doing. A lovely, young lady named Irene had told me her husband was working late and she'd be at her sister's place where she suggested I drop by to see her. The invitation was not subtle, especially since I'd been having an affair with Irene.

That evening, I went out on the pretense of getting a paper to check the horses and promptly went to see Irene at her sister's apartment, only five minutes away. Her sister knew about our affair, and we'd met there before. I had barely sat down and started talking with them when the doorbell rang.

Irene called, "Who is it?" through the closed door.

It was her husband, Sid!

"Nat, quick, hide in the closet," Irene whispered urgently. "I'll get Sid out of here."

Stuffed between two warm coats while balanced on top of boots and umbrellas, I listened. I heard Sid say he'd got off early and brought them ice cream. Irene told him she didn't feel well. "Leave the ice cream," she told her husband. "Please, let's get the hell home."

Sid took Irene home, and I emerged from the stuffy closet. Irene's sister and I enjoyed the tasty chocolate and vanilla ice cream.

Another time, during the ill-fated affair of Nat and Irene, she asked me to come over to her sister's apartment for the afternoon. Irene's brother-in-law was a television camera man, and he often invited his wife to join him on out-of-town shoots, leaving their apartment empty. Irene's job was to water her sister's plants while they were away, which made it very convenient for us to spend the afternoon together. I took off work and joined Irene at the apartment. She told me she had to be home by six o'clock, when her husband was due back from work. I was expected home for dinner by seven.

Around five o'clock, after spending a romantic afternoon together, we kissed goodbye and prepared to leave--only to discover we could not open the door. The freakin' lock broke inside the handle, and it refused to budge. We were trapped! There was only one door, not even a fire escape to climb down. We tried to call the building superintendent and couldn't reach him. Irene grew frantic as time went on and she realized she was late. Finally, with no other options in sight, Irene called her husband at home and explained she was locked in her sister's apartment and couldn't get out. Sid said he'd be right over to help.

By this time, I'd become pretty familiar with that coat closet, so I grimaced when Irene said, "Nat, get in the closet. You can leave after we're gone."

"Whatever you do, don't screw the door up so I can't get out," I warned her as I kicked a boot out of the way, then slid the closet door closed behind me. I stood in the darkness, waiting and listening. It sounded as if Sid practically broke the door down, but he got it open. When I knew the coast was clear, I tried the door. Thankfully, it opened and I made it home, otherwise I'd have been a dead man.

After that, I saw Irene almost every day. I even wanted to marry her, but she loved her husband and wouldn't divorce him. Sid was a good looking man in the commercial photography business who treated her well. Our affair couldn't last. Ultimately, I told Irene if she wouldn't get a divorce I wouldn't see her anymore. She called me about a month later and suggested we get together, "once more for the road." We did--another nice memory--then I never spoke to her again.

Three years ago, I heard through a mutual friend, a lawyer in Suffolk County, that Irene had passed away. "Oh well, such is life," I said to myself, briefly dusting off fond memories.

14

Changing Fortunes

When we came out of the Army, my brother, Morton, and I had about $3,500 between us--*all the money we had in the world*--and we started a business with it. In those days, people bought new homes as fast as you could build them. There wasn't enough housing, and I saw a need. Building was a necessity. We bought two building lots in New York on the waterfront in Bell Harbor. I had saved money from the railroad and borrowed more from the National City Bank around the corner. We built two houses on the corner of Crunston Avenue and 129th Street in Bell Harbor and sold them.

My father was a builder and, as a boy, I had learned a little about building houses before he died, when I was sixteen. I contend that any man, woman, or child who has a brain in their head can become anything they want by studying, copying, using their heads, and starting from the bottom and working their way up. My brother and I knew very little about building, but we risked all our money and started. If you're a good businessman, you don't need to know everything about what you're doing. You can use your head and learn how to manufacture match sticks or make clothing or build houses. In the beginning, I didn't know about building. My ultimate success as a builder is a good example--*a true story of someone using his head and his business sense to make it.*

While building the first two houses, I considered other ventures. I was looking for other business opportunities besides ticket selling at the railroad--something of my own, a way to make more money. At one point I decided to manufacture coats, and I even set up a corporate entity to do so. I planned to knock off my competitors' products--the other guy would make a fantastic coat, and I would make a copy for the knockoff store. They called me "Mr. Knockoff." I almost went into the coat business with a friend who was already in it, but decided not to.

As Morton and I continued to build houses, we ran into trouble. Our houses were too fancy, too expensive, and we had a considerable amount of money tied up in them. Luckily, I had remained with the railroad and still had a sizable income from all my wheeling and dealing there. We sweated bullets when we realized the market couldn't support our houses, but in the end we were able to unload our properties profitably. We had started out with thirty-five hundred dollars and doubled our money in eighteen months. I stopped building houses then, but my brother continued. However, my building days weren't over, and I would later build many more houses and move on to commercial buildings and other developments.

Ultimately, my days with the railroad would come to an end. By that time, I would be thirty-something, still married to my first wife, Fay, and settled down, at least a little.

I almost lost that lucrative job earlier though. It was right after the war, and we didn't have our own place then. We temporarily lived with my mother-in-law and Fay's sister, Sylvia, in their Brooklyn apartment. We returned to New York after a belated honeymoon, a week in Canada. When we walked through the door, my mother-in-law warned, "Nat, you're in big trouble. I think you lost your job."

"What do you mean, I lost my job?" I couldn't see how that was possible, certain she didn't know what she was talking about. "I'm supposed to go in to work on Tuesday."

My mother-in-law tried to explain. "While you were away, Sylvia was fired."

Sylvia worked for Warner Brothers. She was in their transportation department, driving actors and actresses around and arranging for their transportation all over the country. I'd needed to buy extra space on the trains with the winter travel season approaching, so I'd asked Sylvia to reserve a whole list of spaces in Warner Brothers' name. After all, I figured they were Warner Brothers and could get anything they wanted.

"What happened?" I asked.

"Sylvia was fired because of you," accused my mother-in-law.

Sylvia was just a kid, younger than Fay, and knew nothing of what I was doing. One day, while she was out to lunch, the Pennsylvania Railroad called her office to confirm all the space she'd asked for. I had been speculating again, reserving space I thought I could use--Pullman space, apartments, drawing rooms, roomettes for destinations all over the country, particularly Florida and Hollywood. Sylvia's assistant took the call while she was out and told the railroad that Warner Brothers hadn't ordered those spaces. When Sylvia returned, she confessed everything and they fired her on the spot. I felt bad, very sorry that I'd gotten her fired.

Fortunately, Warner Brothers hired her back again a few days later. Meanwhile, I suspected I was in trouble now. My boss at the railroad was likely waiting for me to come back to work. Sure enough, the minute I showed up I was called into Fred Loeffel's office. He asked me what I was doing with the space.

"What space?" I denied everything.

Then I called Charlie Reeves from the union, told him what I'd done, and asked his advice. "Do you want to represent me?" I asked.

"No," he said, "I can't go in and represent you at trial if you're going to lie. You go in there and deny every God-damned thing. Tell them it's all lies."

They put me on trial, just like court. I went in front of Loeffel and Horsch, and they questioned me. I told those gentlemen that I knew nothing about it and that if my sister-in-law told them anything, she was telling an untruth. It went on and on like that, her word against mine.

I knew I was dead when the trial notes were typed up and they asked me to sign the testimony I'd given. I called Charlie from the union. "Charlie, I can't sign the papers because when I sign, I'm swearing to it."

He said, "If you can't, you will have to hand in your resignation. You will be fired if you don't sign."

I shrugged. "Well, okay, f--k it. I'm building houses anyway, so I'll quit."

But you know what? They never came to me with that form to sign. I stayed with the railroad for several more years until I got my building business well underway to success. But that's another chapter . . . .

15

Married Life, Children, and Building a Business

I concentrated on making a good living out of my job at the railroad and tried to find an apartment where Fay and I could settle into married life and start a family. The first house Morton and I had built in Bell Harbor was sold to a man who had been renting an apartment in Brooklyn. When he bought the house, I grabbed at the chance to take over renting his Brooklyn apartment--finally a place of our own! Apartments were so hard to get that landlords had a good thing going. Too good. Our landlord was such a thief. I paid him five hundred dollars under the table just to get the place, then he raised our rent. Five hundred dollars was a lot of money at that time. The apartment was in a beautiful building and, although only one bedroom, it had a good sized kitchen, living room, dining room and one and a half baths. The rent was forty-three dollars a month.

Fay wanted kids. It took almost five years from the beginning of our marriage for her to become pregnant. She gave birth to our first child, Charles, by cesarean section on April 30, 1948. Two years later, Fay was pregnant again and we had a second son, Geoffrey, born June 30, 1951. The brothers were three years apart in age.

Well, now I had two children, so I *really* needed to make more money, and the apartment was getting pretty small for my growing family. I was still working for the railroad, making good money, and I had a few dollars put away. My brother was building houses on his own. I considered getting back into the building business and started to look around for property. I found a piece of property in Seaford, Long Island on which I could build thirteen houses. I went to see the owner, Joe Hanson, a lovely gentleman who had retired from his job as head bookkeeper for Reingold Breweries, a large, well-known brewery in Brooklyn, and was moving to Riviera Beach, Florida. After we met and hit it off, he dropped his price on the house from fifty thousand to forty-five thousand because he thought I was "a nice fellah," much to the dismay of his furious wife.

The house, a brick, two-story, English Tudor with three bedrooms was on a beautiful plot of land. Huge blue spruce trees lined the path from the street to the front door. I saw the potential in this piece of land and fell in love with it. What would it take to build the housing development I envisioned here?

There were several problems, not the least of which was money. This perfect house was in the middle of this great piece of property. It wasn't divided into plots; there was no landscaping, no hookups, no building plans. Hanson gave me a land survey which I had checked out by a surveyor and engineer. That night, I unrolled the survey on my dining room table and studied it to figure out where I'd put in cesspools (there were no sewers), curbs, sidewalks, landscaping. I didn't have the money for the purchase of the Tudor, let alone what it would cost to develop the property.

The next day I met with Hanson and his wife and made them an offer of $40,000. The woman went crazy and threw me out of their house. I don't think I've ever met any woman who was as rough as Hanson's wife.

He was embarrassed by her behavior, and I walked away feeling very disappointed. I desperately wanted to buy that house and property.

I feared I couldn't afford to buy the house and land I'd fallen in love with. My building dreams were nearly thwarted. To buy a piece of property like this one, no matter what the cost, you had to have money. Who the hell had $45,000 in their pocket, or even $42,000? I certainly didn't have that kind of cash from working nights at the railroad. But I had business sense, guts, and determination. Angry at myself for provoking Mrs. Hanson and blowing the deal, I decided to go and see the old man and offer him $42,000. But his wife wouldn't let me in the front door. She wouldn't even talk to me and refused to let me talk with her husband. I turned away again in frustration and disappointment.

Like a dog with a bone, I wouldn't give up and kept driving by the property and looking at the house. Several days later, lo and behold, there was Mr. Hanson sitting on the front steps! I pulled the car off to the side and parked along the curb. I walked up to Joe Hanson, took a deep breath and said, "I changed my mind. I'll give you $42,000 for the house."

He raised his brows. "You will?"

I nodded. "Yeah." As I uttered the word, I knew I only had $14,000 to my name.

I wanted that Tudor house and that property so bad. I saw the possibility for building thirteen more houses there and strongly believed the project would be a huge financial success, the beginning of my new career, and the perfect answer for my growing family. Mr. Hanson agreed to sell it to me for $42,000. I don't know what he told his wife.

Now I simply had to come up with the money . . . . *Where was I going to find it?*

With strong vision, a stubborn nature, and charged with energy, I set out to find solutions to the problems standing in my way. Even before I'd begun my building project in Seaford, I knew I was going to be short of money. I was madly trying to make ends meet, working day and night at the railroad and on building plans, and putting all I had into the project. Everything was a challenge, a feat of engineering, a never-ending struggle to find more money. Throughout the struggle, I always kept my goal in mind, and avenues opened to get me what I wanted.

While building the first two houses in Bell Harbor, I had met a nice, elderly gentleman with the Security Tile Company who'd taken a liking to my brother and me. He'd told us then that if we ever had a problem we should come to him and he'd help us out. Now at twenty-nine years old, with a wife and two kids, and needing a lot of money, I called him with quite a big problem. He knew a retired builder who was chairman of the County Federal Savings and Loan at Rockville Center and was happy to introduce me to the banker.

I explained what I needed money-wise and offered to show the banker the property. He was seventy-five years old and spoke with a Swedish accent. "Son, come with me and show me," the banker said.

I was amazed when he led me to his car, which was at least twenty-eight years old. My car, which had cost me three hundred dollars, was a Rolls Royce in comparison. We climbed in and I was surprised that the old clunker actually made the half-hour trip to Seaford, even though it sputtered all the way.

The banker liked the property, and the *builder* in him saw the possibilities. He also liked me and my ideas; perhaps I reminded him of his own younger days. "It looks good," he said. "Tell you what. Let's go back to the bank and we work out a deal."

Back at the bank, he called Jerry in the mortgage office (with his Swedish accent it sounded like *Cheddy*). "Cheddy, come in here right away," the banker said. "I've got a nice young kid here. He wants to build houses and we got to help him. We got to give him mortgages on those houses."

When a builder builds homes and people buy them, they do so with a mortgage. Jerry had a mortgage office and was vice president of the bank. That day, he shook my hand. "Come in with a set of plans, and we'll give you a mortgage," he offered.

And so began a long association between Jerry and myself. He became my banker for many years, and I became the successful builder I wanted to be. Jerry was very good to me and, when I later had a disagreement over rates, he left that bank and I followed him to another.

To clarify: I actually got that first mortgage from Jerry on the *Tudor house I was buying*, not the land. In those days, you couldn't get a mortgage on vacant land. The purchase price was $42,000, so I arranged a mortgage for $25,000 for the house. That was the top price you could get a mortgage for on any house in those days. I combined that with my own savings of $14,000 and came up with $39,000--just $6,000 short of what I needed to pay Mr. Hanson and his lovely wife. Undaunted, I borrowed $2,200 from my sister-in-law, Sylvia, and $2,000 from my brother-in-law, Jack Tannenbaum. Because I worked for the railroad, National City Bank extended me a loan for an additional $2,000, which I wouldn't have to pay back for several years. I also borrowed off my GI insurance. Now I had money to maneuver.

I completed the deal to buy the Tudor house and the Seaford property. Next, I needed to draw up a set of plans. I knew that the best way to become successful in business was by following in the footsteps of another successful person in the same business. I looked around at other developments to see which ones were doing best. I interviewed other developers and analyzed what they were doing.

To build a house, the first thing I had to do was dig a hole and put in a foundation. I hired subcontractors--plumbers, bricklayers, carpenters, painters, electricians, roofers. I wasn't only the developer, I was also the general contractor. I had no professional contractor because they required thirteen percent. I had no money to give them; I did my own building.

16

Family Life

By this time, I had two kids and realized I needed a proper house for my family, a home to raise young children in, with a back yard where they could play. So, in addition to my Seaford development property, I purchased a two-family house in Lynbrook, Long Island. Originally, it had been a single-family, two-story dwelling, but the previous owner had converted the upstairs into a separate apartment. The house cost me $14,000 (the same house today would cost $300,000). I moved Fay and the kids into that house with a GI mortgage, and although a down payment was not required, I managed to put $1,000 down. GI mortgages were at five percent, and my stint with the Army entitled me to the insurance.

I rented the upstairs for a hundred dollars a month to an elderly retired couple, lovely people. That hundred dollars paid all my house expenses: mortgage payment, electric and fuel bills. I cut the grass and did the landscaping myself, planting beautiful flowers in the yard. We never locked the house, and the couple upstairs never locked their apartment. In the early 1950s nobody locked the doors of their homes--in fact, most doors didn't even have locks on them--and nobody ever stole anything.

I'd always planned to have children. Being a father was an important and rewarding part of my life. However, I worked seven days a week and didn't spend as much time with my children as I would have liked. I made my share of mistakes as a parent. For the first eighteen months while I got my building business going and developed the Seaford property, I also kept up my job selling tickets at the railroad. I was far too busy for any family life, and raising the children at that time was pretty much left to Fay.

Over the years, I didn't take a lot of vacations with my family, but I occasionally took a three- or four-day weekend, and we'd go Puerto Rico and enjoy the beach there, swim in the ocean with the kids. I did make it to most of my sons' little league games, and at one point, I even managed a couple of their baseball teams that played against each other.

Both the boys were born blonde, but by the time they reached the age of two, their hair had turned brown. They may have shared hair color as young children, but otherwise, my two sons were very different from each other. Geoffrey was built much stockier than Charles. Charles was quiet, while Geoffrey was always more boisterous and outgoing.

From the time they were nine or ten until their early teens, the boys went to camp during the summers and really enjoyed it. Every summer, Fay and I visited them at the camp, a beautiful lakeside acreage in upstate New York.

The boys worked during time off from school. Just as I had learned about work from my father when he hired me to sweep up in his building projects, I hired my sons to sweep rubbish out of the houses I built. Many of my houses were two-story, so I had to be careful they didn't get hurt, but by age twelve they were able to handle the job. And just as I had learned the value of education from my mother, I passed that knowledge along to my children. Both boys graduated from high school and went on to college.

Right after they finished college Charles and Geoff began working with me. I thought it proper at the time, and their mother did too, but I discovered it was a mistake. I simply wanted to give them an opportunity to see what I did. In retrospect, I think doing this made it too easy for them. I feel they should have gone out and found their own jobs after graduation, learned about other opportunities and worked for someone else for two or three years before joining me. I want to tell successful young people in business that when their children get out of school, they ought to get a job somewhere else first.

17

Partnership: From Residential to Commercial

You never know someone until you live with them--and that means people in business, too. Now, I had just purchased the Seaford property with the Tudor house on it, *the ideal spot for my dream housing development.* Before I put a shovel to the ground, I reworked my figures and decided I needed an additional ten thousand dollars to make the project go without cutting my throat in the process. As a business man, you have to learn how to add and subtract and face what those numbers tell you. I needed a partner.

Back when I had built my first two houses in Bell Harbor, I ran into a man by the name of Ike Elias, a dress manufacturer-come-builder who had a few extra dollars. He lived in a fancy neighborhood on the ocean, up the block from where Morton and I had built our houses. One day in 1947, Elias had stopped by our building site on Crunston Avenue to have a look. "Hey boys, you're doing pretty good here," he said, after introducing himself. "I'm building a couple of houses myself, but my partner doesn't know much about the building business. You two fellahs are okay. If you ever run into problems and need a partner, give me a call."

That had been four years earlier. By this time, Ike Elias had a big office with two other partners, all large investors. I picked up the phone . . . . I remember the moment vividly.

"Mr. Elias," I began, my voice sounding surprisingly calm despite the pulse pounding in my ears, "I'm Nat Serota, the one who built the two homes on Crunston Avenue. You remember me?"

He remembered me and was very willing to listen to my proposal. To make a long story short, Elias and I became business partners, and my Seaford venture was a huge success. I sold the brick Tudor house alone for $25,000, after having paid $42,000 for the house and all the land. That meant I had invested just $17,000 for thirteen plots of land on which I built and sold thirteen more houses. Those houses, each about 22,000 square feet on quarter-acre plots, sold for a base price of $15, 990, and all were sold within three months. The original Tudor is still there today, and so are the ones I built around it.

Pleased with my success, I remarked to my partner that if I could continue to make $500 a week I could live like a king for the rest of my life. That was the beginning of my growth as a successful developer and a testament to my philosophy that anyone can make it, anyone can make that extra buck. Anyone can succeed--a candy store owner or someone running a clothing store--if they are smart. You can't grow unless you use your head. And at eighty-one years old at the time of this writing, I'm still growing today. I still have two or three jobs cooking at any given time. I've still got problems--there are always problems in any business and in life--but I think them through and find solutions, use my head, and talk with others who use their heads.

Back in the beginning, Ike Elias and I embarked on a successful business partnership, starting with our first housing development, the thirteen houses on my property in Seaford beside the Tudor house. We then built a second development in a different area of Seaford, this one with thirty-nine houses. From there, we went on to build 200 single-family homes in Hewlett, Long Island. After that, we built sixty-nine houses in Woodmere, in the five-town area, on sand land that had been filled in. We continued to build houses for six years.

Building houses was a tough business because once built, you had to sell them to the public. A couple shopping for a home, for example, would come by on the weekend with fourteen kids, aunts, uncles, and grandparents. All those people would drive me crazy. They'd finally decide to buy the home, but then they'd want to make design changes, then more changes, and on and on. It's not that we couldn't make any money selling houses, but it drove us crazy. When we got into the more controlled and lucrative business of building commercial buildings, we quit building houses entirely and started making real money.

Business was booming. The shopping center and commercial building business was different in that we kept the buildings rather than selling them; the shopping centers became part of our business empire. Today, I still own the first shopping center that I built forty years ago. It's on the corner of Peninsula Boulevard and Mill Road in Hewlett, Long Island--The Hewlett Shopping Center. I built another shopping center half a mile further along Peninsula Boulevard, in the next little town in a string of towns. One featured the Big Apple Supermarket, and the other had a Waldbaum's Supermarket. I built the first Big Apple on Long Island.

To build a shopping center, first we'd buy a piece of land and erect a large building so we could rent it to a supermarket chain; then we'd build other stores alongside it. The supermarket was always the drawing card for the shopping center; it brought people in every day and spread business to the other stores. Ultimately, in my total career as a builder, I built some forty odd shopping centers.

To further explain my business: As a developer, I buy a piece of property for X amount of dollars. I put up Y dollars in cash and take a mortgage for the rest. The person who sold me the land got ten, twenty or thirty percent up front, and the rest was held as a first mortgage. The developer gets the title (I have never paid all cash to get a land title) and becomes the first mortgagee and must begin building. A developer can't get any money from a bank until he has built the foundation, put in the steel, brickwork, and so on. In the meantime, the bank gives me a commitment for a first mortgage, a structural first mortgage, or a permanent first mortgage, which could be a twenty- or thirty-year mortgage.

Let's assume you're a developer and you owe the landowner a million dollars. The bank is ready to give you, say, a million and a half. The first million they give you at closing goes to pay the landowner and the rest goes to you. It is from that money that the developer pays the contractors as the project goes along. As you do more work, and therefore show more development, you apply to the bank for more money. You can have a first mortgage, a second mortgage, and sometimes a third. The bank, as the first mortgagee, always pays the landowner off first.

When I was building the Shirley Shopping Center, halfway through the project I bought other land on which I planned to build another shopping center, then another, and then another. That's how I have forty odd shopping centers. But you can't start a construction job like that unless you have some tenants lined up, major tenants like a supermarket or department store. Otherwise, a builder had better not put a shovel to the ground. The rest of the property will be rented as you go along, but you must have that major tenant in place at the start. When you complete the whole shopping center, you are usually left with twenty percent of the space still available, but that's okay, because when the center opens, the space gets rented.

In those days, it didn't take long to get a building permit--only a few days--while today it takes a year or two to get a permit to even start. You can't even knock a God-damned tree down on your own property without a permit today. When I was building the houses in Hempstead (Seaford and Woodmere are in Hempstead), an original set of plans cost around two hundred dollars per house, and every set of duplicate plans cost twenty-five dollars. To get the permits issued, I took the plans to the building inspector, Mr. Curry. I brought him anywhere from fifteen to forty plans at once, each with changes in the colors for the brick or woodwork or shutters and so on.

"Hey kid, when do you need these?" Mr. Curry asked.

Without batting an eye, I said, "I need them right away."

"Come in tomorrow around three o'clock, and I'll have them all ready for ya." I couldn't believe he'd have that much ready in such a short time, but he did. Life is so different today; now you have to wait for everything.

Ike Elias and I remained business partners for twenty-five years. (Ike was ten years older and we split when he wanted to retire.) Ike was a nice guy, and he'd made a lot of money, but he had a lot of trouble in his life. He had two sons, just as I did, but sadly, he lost one of his sons to drugs. When that happened, Ike became very distressed and wanted out of our partnership.

We remained partners for some time on the shopping centers and the buildings we owned jointly, even after we'd stopped building together. Eventually, we auctioned off our joint properties. We ended up in court for almost eight years fighting each other. At the end of the whole battle, Ike was out over a million dollars in legal fees, and my costs were nearly that as well. I found him impossible to deal with in the end, and we literally didn't speak to each other for a long time.

After the partnership broke up, I continued to build office buildings and shopping centers. Today, at eighty-one years old, I'm still doing it and don't plan to retire. In addition to buildings, I also built many relationships through the years while doing business in and around the New York area. I have seen a lot of people come and go and many things change.

Some years ago, one of the biggest kingpins in the supermarket business on the East Coast was Atlantic-Pacific (A & P), but I couldn't do business with them. They had an elderly gentleman in charge of real estate who never gave a landlord more than a five-year lease. Whenever I found a commercial parcel on which I wanted to build, I'd call this man to tell him I'd found a perfect location for an A & P, but I always needed more than a five-year lease.

He always said, "No, Serota. We only sign for five years."

And each time I replied, "Well, forget about it. Goodbye."

Some of Atlantic-Pacific's competitors became very successful because I found these great locations and, as a landlord, gave them twenty-year leases. With a twenty-year lease I got a longer mortgage and a better profit on the bottom line, so I made more money from the other supermarkets. I built especially good relationships with the Big Apple Supermarket, H.C. Bohack (another chain of small stores), and Waldbaum's.

As Waldbaum's business grew, my business grew, and I came to know Ira Waldbaum well. Ira was six years my junior. I had known his father in the supermarket business in Brooklyn. Those original supermarkets were only five thousand square feet, like postage stamps compared to the superstores of today. When I bought a piece of property that I thought would suit Waldbaum's, I called Ira to negotiate a deal. I rented the building to Waldbaum's at two dollars and twenty-five cents a foot, and that was good money then. How things have changed! Today, we get anywhere from fifteen to twenty dollars a foot for a supermarket. The shopping centers I build now can bring in up to half to a million dollars, depending on size. That first Waldbaum's Center I built was only 17,000 square feet, but it was the biggest supermarket on the island at the time. In contrast, today our supermarkets are anywhere from 40,000 to 75,000 square feet, and that's two to four times as large.

Forty years ago, nobody imagined such size; I was happy with the first deal I made with Ira Waldbaum and so was he. After that, I introduced myself to Artie Zuckerman, knowing he was in the supermarket business with Big Apple, and asked if he wanted me to build one for him. We made a deal, and I ended up building three or four Big Apple Supermarkets. Zuckerman was just the opposite of Ira Waldbaum. You had to watch out for Artie. However, once you knew that, you knew how to do business with him. You simply overcame him by playing the game of "if he thought he was screwing you, then you could screw him back."

I used to make deals on a handshake in those days, because everybody was basically honest. I worked with Mel Weiss, who was a straight shooter, and president of Big Apple under Artie. Zuckerman eventually sold his company for eight million dollars--which was an absolute fortune at the time--and screwed Weiss in the process. Mel Weiss was a brilliant businessman and a hard-working guy with a vision; he soon went into business for himself and became an astounding success. In the end, he sold his own business for millions more than Zuckerman had sold Big Apple for. Mel recently retired and now lives about five minutes away from me in Florida with his sweet wife, Ellen.

One of my biggest projects was the Times Square Stores. I built several shopping centers for them, working with the owner, George Seedman, many times. He was a hard bargainer and not an easy man to deal with, but I had the prime locations he wanted. Seedman was a true character, and I came to know him well. Tall and thin, he was married and divorced three times (I went to two of his weddings). Before he decided to marry for a fourth and final time, George asked for my opinion of his future bride, a lovely young woman with two children.

I used to laugh at George--secretly, because you couldn't laugh *at* him. I still remember the first time I met him over lunch; he was sixty-five (which I thought was terribly old then) and made an admiring remark about the pretty blonde seated at a nearby table. I remember laughing with my partner over the elderly Seedman still having an eye for the ladies. Little did I know then that, even at eighty-one, so would I.

Once, Seedman and I had an argument over a deal. I told him off, and he refused to talk to me for months, but he never backed out of our agreement because he was a sharp businessman and knew the location was good. I continued to build his store, even though he wasn't speaking to me. On opening day, he showed up and I congratulated him on his new store. Suddenly, we were on speaking terms again.

Some time later, after he'd backed out of a deal to sell all his stores for fifty million dollars, I offered him thirty-five million for them, but he refused to sell to me because he claimed I'd made enough money already. He ultimately sold out for seventeen million to a company that liquidated the stores, but not before sending them a letter saying how difficult his landlord, Nat Serota, was to deal with. Seedman passed away a few years ago at the age of ninety-nine.

People are very difficult but very funny. It was a wonderful life dealing with all kinds of people and doing business with them. There was never a dull moment, always lots to laugh about and lots to yell about.

Great Eastern Mills had one of the first discount houses in New Jersey. They came to me, wanting me to build them a store on Long Island so they could rent it. Their merchandise was very, very cheap, and Great Eastern was successful, both because of that and because of how their operation was run. There were five partners involved--one ran the business, hands-on in the supermarket and discount department store--and they made millions. When I told them how much the rent would be, they went crazy. They were more comfortable in a partnership, thus spreading the risk, so, since it was *only a couple of bucks*, we decided to become partners with them in the Long Island store.

My part in the deal was to find the location--a sensational location and a very expensive property. It always took money to get the very best. Most of the land I bought for building was at top cost because of location. I bought twenty-five acres on which to build the Great Eastern Mills store, paying $125,000 an acre, an unheard of price at that time. It was actually a crazy, risky move then. We owned twenty-two percent of that discount store, but it was an unbelievably successful venture. It was the only time I ever became a partner in a store rather than just being the landlord.

I also built Alexander's Department Store, which was owned by George Farkas. It became a huge success, one of the largest department stores in New York City.

Commercial building is a continuous process. When you buy a piece of property, you have to analyze it--as a landlord, you decide who it might suit--and on that basis, you buy it. While you are building one shopping center, you are buying other properties and talking to various people to see who might want them. The supermarket business has boomed over the last forty years, and all of my shopping centers are anchored by a big supermarket.

I could write fourteen books about my business dealings, but the long story wouldn't be so short then. The building business has been, and remains, a large part of my life. Like in any business, you have thieves, nice people and . . . well, you know. The same with contractors--some are excellent and some aren't. You have to be smart enough to figure out who is best. It's a game and you take risks. You have to understand and accept the bad with the good.

18

The Auction

The City of New York owned a piece of property right in front of Green Acres Mall, the number one shopping center in the country at that time, on the borderline between Nassau County and Brooklyn. Brooklyn had sales tax and Nassau County did not. This prime piece of city-owned, no-tax property--9.2 acres in front of Green Acres--came up for sale at auction. It was only two or three minutes from our office, and I'd had my eye on it. At the auction they set an upset price, which meant it couldn't be sold for any less. The upset price for this property was very high for the standards of the day--$1,750,000! I was still in partnership with Eias at this time, and I urged him, "Let's get on that. We can build stores there, and we'll knock 'em dead."

There had been water wells on the property which supplied water to the mains in the area. The City of New York no longer needed the water, so they cut off the mains and redirected a supply from elsewhere. More importantly, the city needed the money from the sale of this property. They had the village of Valley Stream change the zoning to commercial/retail and worked out a deal whereby they got the zoning changed so the village would get forty percent of the sale price, while the city, which owned the land, would get sixty percent of the sale price.

Excitedly, I rushed to show Ike the figures I had worked out. I'd figured out how much it would cost to build and how much rent we could get. The location was superb. The point is that it was *the best in America*. I'm not joking. It was even better than the best locations we already owned for the Times Square Stores. We decided we could afford to bid as high as $2,500,000 at auction for the Green Acres property.

A couple of months before the auction, I applied for the necessary bidding forms and we met the broker in New York. Thinking I had a good chance to win the bid, Lenny Goldberg wanted to make a deal with me. I agreed that I'd list his name as the broker on the sale, which would give him $100,000 in commission, then he'd kick half of it back to me, so, in effect, the property would cost me $50,000 less.

On the day of the auction, my partner and I chose not to drive into the city. We took the train to Penn Station, me joking that it felt like I was going to my old office at the railroad. During the train ride, all I could think about was the auction, who would be bidding against us and how high would they go. I turned to Ike and said over the hum of the train, "We can go as high as $3,000,000."

He shook his head. "I'm not going for $3,000,000. If you want to bid that much, you go ahead and bid it. If you're short of money, I'll give you what you need, but I don't want to be partners for $3,000,000."

"Okay," I said. If the bid got higher than what we'd agreed upon, it was my choice to continue, and I understood I'd be on my own.

We crossed the road from Penn Station and entered the Pennsylvania Hotel. The Grand Ballroom was noisy with the chaotic chatter of at least a thousand people waiting for the auction to begin. We found seats in the large ballroom. A fast-talking auctioneer, just like you see on television, took verbal bids rather than sealed bids. I had a long wait. The property I wanted was last on a list of fifty to sixty other pieces of property.

The air in the room was charged with excitement as people shouted out their bids. While I waited in anticipation, I ran into some lawyers I knew. I admitted my interest in the Green Acres property when they asked me why I was there. They told me they were just there to watch, but I knew they were lying. One of the lawyers worked for Alexander's Department Store. The Green Acres Mall, over a hundred acres of shopping, was already home to many of the big department stores. I could appreciate what an important and sensational location that very piece of property in front of the mall would be to a store like Alexander's.

At last the auctioneer announced the 9.2 acres I wanted, starting the bidding at the absolutely unheard of price of $1,750,000. For a long moment the hush in the room was audible. I broke the silence with my bid. That unleashed a fervor of bidding which lasted for over an hour. As the auctioneer took fifty-five bids, I hung in with resolute determination. The winning bid was $3,441,000. It was mine!

The rule at this auction was that you had to put ten percent down immediately after winning a bid. I had already arranged with my banker to cover my check. As I made my way forward to write the check, people clamored around me.

"Hey Serota," someone called, "Who've ya got?"

"I got nobody," I said.

"Well, how in hell are you going to pay this kind of money?"

"Just relax," I told them with a smile. "I know what I'm doing."

My purchase was big news, reported in all the papers--*The Herald Tribune, The New York Times*. The following morning, I got a call from Irwin Channin, an elderly gentleman of about seventy who owned the whole Green Acres Shopping Center. (Everything behind my new piece of property belonged to him.) He asked to see me.

Irwin was a big-time builder who'd had his share of ups and downs. He was almost completely blind, and his two sons worked in the business with him. His office was at the top of the Channin building on East 42nd Street, which he'd built about forty years earlier. That is where I went to meet him. It was a tremendous office, but the peeling paint on the walls made me wonder if it had been painted in the last thirty years.

I sat down at the end of his big desk and asked, "What can I do for you?"

Channin got right to the point. "I want that piece, and I'll give you a profit."

"What do you mean? I bought it to build on."

"Don't get excited. I want the piece, and I'll give you $600,000 profit on it right now," he offered calmly. I quickly calculated the profit in my mind. I'd paid three million, four, forty-one. He wanted to pay me four million and change.

"Well, Mr. Channin," I said, "I've got to pay taxes."

"Yeah, I knew you were going to tell me that, Serota. But I've thought about this and I tell you what I'm going to do for ya. I own all those apartments behind Green Acres. We'll work out a deal. I'll give you the apartments, so you'll have an income. But *I want that piece*," he insisted.

"Tell you what, Mr. Channin, I'll think about it." I left his office, walking on air with conflicting thoughts swirling in my mind. I hadn't hung on through all that bidding and won that property *not to build on it*. But $600,000 was a lot of money.

I returned to my office and sat down with Ike to talk it through. "What do I want with apartments and all the headaches that go with them?" I finally resolved. I waited four days, then called Channin to tell him the property was not for sale. I was going to build!

Channin swore he'd fight me in court and stop me from building. When I asked him how he could possibly fight me, he replied, "I know reasons why that zoning change deal should never have been made by

Valley Stream and the city."

"Well, you have to do what you have to do," I said politely. "See you in court."

19

Enjoying the Battle

The presiding judge was famous on the stand of the Supreme Court in Nassau County. I had hired a top law firm from New York, Paul Weiss Rifkin. I sat in the front row with my lawyers, primed and ready to fight. The court was called to order. Suddenly, a tall, thin man with snow-white hair stood up. I recognized him as the head man who'd bid against me at the auction. When the bidding started, there were about ten people bidding, but as the price went up, most had dropped out. This man had not.

"Your Honor, I'd like to speak as a friend of the court," said the white-haired man. "I'd like to tell you about this piece of property which should *never* have been sold to Mr. Serota."

I jumped up from the middle of the front row, with my lawyers still seated. "Your Honor, this man is not a friend of the court." After the auction, I had made it my business to find out that this white-haired man who'd bid against me was a lawyer representing Mr. Channin.

The judge looked down at me from the bench. "Who are you?"

"I'm Serota. I'm the man who got the property at the auction. We are here in this courtroom today because Mr. Channin wants this property and doesn't want me to build on it. Please ask this man, *as a friend of the court*, if he was present at the auction."

"Why?" asked the judge.

"Just ask him who he represented at the auction."

"That's a good point," said the judge, and he turned to the white-haired man. "Were you at the auction?"

"Yeah," said the man.

"Your Honor, ask him if he was bidding," I prompted.

After the man admitted he'd been bidding, the judge asked him who he'd been bidding for.

"I was bidding for Mr. Channin."

"Then you're not a friend of this court. Sit down!" demanded the judge.

I won that case.

As I reflect on my life now, I have to say that I had a good time *every day*. I usually came out the winner in court cases, and I *always* enjoyed a good battle. Only one time I came close to losing a court case. Actually, I was sentenced to five years, but didn't have to serve it because I was found innocent, and the case was thrown out of court.

The case with Channin was big news, and I have lots of articles regarding that story.

The very next day after I won the case and could begin construction, George Farkas of Alexander's Department Store walked into my office with his lawyer. As it turned out, he'd had a deal with Channin to build, but Channin didn't get the property. I did.

So, Farkas and his lawyer sat in my office and we talked dollars and cents. They wanted a big building, more than three hundred thousand square feet. Alexander's Department Store was on a par with Macy's--very important in the retail market. A little guy, George Farkas had started a small dry goods business in a basement with no money and eventually became the owner of Alexander's. George was a decent guy, but his lawyer was a nasty son-of-a-bitch. I already knew the man, as he'd sat across a desk from me on many other occasions representing Waldbaum's. By the time I had negotiated ten or twelve leases with Waldbaum's, I came to know this rough lawyer very well.

That day, George Farkas, his lawyer and I sat in my office for hours. We talked and got nowhere. George turned to his lawyer, who was also his personal friend, and said, "Get the hell out of here." When the lawyer left, George and I sat down. We negotiated, compromised, and eventually made a deal, then shook hands on it. Later, after George had left my office, his lawyer called to tell me the deal was off.

I shrugged and said, "Who the hell are you? I'm going to build my stores."

A week later, I placed an ad in the paper showing that I was going to build in front of Green Acres. The morning it appeared, George Farkas called me. "Serota, I'll be in to see you at two o'clock to make a deal with you."

That afternoon we made another deal, but George had forgotten the dollar figure we had originally agreed upon, so without realizing it, he gave me an extra $50,000 a year. George and I became good friends anyway and would work together often in the future.

Family Photo: Maternal Grandparents
My greatgrandmother is sitting in middle of photo; my grandfather sitting on far right and grandmother on the left. My mother is standing in the back (middle).

My father

My mother

Nat in the buggy

Nat, riding in front

"Nucky" Nuckam at about four, taking a pee in front of a building my father built.

Family Photo: I'm in the far back (about 14 years old), behind my mother and father; Morton is in front of me and Rita in front of him. Betty is dressed in black.

Pies I used to bake

Nat, weigh master at the coal yard now seventeen or eighteen

Nat as First Seargent, 1943

In the Army, Nat carries the battalion flag

1977, Deborah, Dena and Daniel
(photo by H&H Photography

The Serota Boys: (L to R) Daniel, Nat, Steve, Johnathan and Chase

Karen Serota

Charles with Jennifer (seven) and Lauren (three), taken in 1985

Son Geoffry; this photo taken in 1983

Vivian's mother and father, Rev. Zue Aroni and Frances, taken approximately 1987 in Florida at her father's concert.

Mitchel Field office building
1982

Valley Stream, around 1968

East Meadow, 1978

Vivian and Nat with Pope John Paul II

Pope John Paul II giving me the wafer

Who's the man next to Vivian and Serota? Behind His Holiness, Pope John Paul II, is Msgr. William O'Brian. Note: Mary Tyler Moore is further to the right, behind her stands Moore's father and mother.

Our first trip to Israel in 1977: Diasapora Museum

His Royal Highness Prince Jean of Luxembourg
Her Royal Highness Princess Maria Beatrice di Savoia
His Royal Highness Prince Dimitri of Yugoslavia

of the International Anti-Drug Abuse Foundation

request the pleasure of your company

at a Valentine Party
on Monday, February 6, 1984
from 6:30 to 9:00 pm

at the home of

Vivian and Nathan L. Serota
895 Park Avenue
New York City

Regrets only
(212) 354-6000 ext. 207

International anti-Drug Program

One of Ben's $2.00 bills

True and best friend, Carl Manis

Nat and Vivian at Kennedy
Center, Washington, D.C. in 1986

Nat and Vivian and
Richard Dryfuss at his
wedding in California
April 1983

1989, Vivian with Nat and Senator Al D'Amoto at the opening of Nat's new offices

Grand Opening for "Top Rollers" around 1979, at the roller skating rink Vivian managed

The late Nathan Pritikin in 1982. Nat and Vivian with Richard Dryfuss

Posing for Playboy -- not really! Cerebal Palsey fundraiser gives all guests their own "Playmate of the Year" photo.

Vivian and Nat on a cruise to Greece around 1983

Ethyl Rayrod, dearest friend of Vivian and Nat who designed Nat's offece and Florida home

Directing traffic in Beijing: Marshall, Diane, and Nat, 1983

Nat modeling oriental wedding robes during their Japan trip

1983 Nat and Vivian, and Marshall and Diane in the Orient

1983 Nat and Vivian on Tienneman Square

Vivian -- gorgeous -- and always a different look!

In the late 1980s we hosted a movie star party: "Come as Your Favorite Movie Star Party!" (left to right) Nat dressed as Nathan Detroit; Ernie and Kelly Anastos, Channel 2 Anchor; Vivian dressed as Rita Hayworth.

"To Nathan, a.k.a. our 'Nathan Detroit." You come across as tough. However, underneath that tough exterior is a heart of gold. Twenty years full of memories, from Boca to Beijing -- from Pritikin to Regine's -- years of travel, talking, laughter, holidays, family gatherings and parties. The song, 'You Can Count On Me' must have been written about you, as we all know how much you care for all your friends and family -- with the deepest love and affection -- and you certainly have ours. Love, Diane Feldstein"

Nancy Reagan, Chair of the ball to raise money for Daytop Village in the mid-eighties. Behind her: Monsignor O'Brien, Nat, and Madame Donna Marie Piar FanFani

During the eighties Daytop Village, 40th Street: Prime Minister FanFani of Italy

(Left to right): Nat, Louise Kornfeld and Al Trenk, Phyllis, in the red hat, Mia in the black hat, and Steven Kornfeld on the right. Taken at Ascot 1997.

Party at our home, April 1992 celebrating Kenny Solms Birthday. (Left to right): Vivian, Ben, Kenny Solms, Dolly Parton and Sandy Galan.

Early '90s, party we hosted for Robert Rauschenberg. (Left to Right): Vivian, Cheryl Lee Terry and Robert Rauschenberg.

Helene and Al Kaplan 1998

Nyril Kahane Haase, 1997

Party at Ivana Trump's apartment (Left to right): Nat, Ivana, Fabio, and Vivian, 1992.

Vivian and Nat at Ivana Trump's birthday party in London

Ann and Arnold Kopelson

August 1998 Buzz Aldrin on my boat in France, *X-Ta-Sea*, a Sunseaker.

Nat, having taken off his hairpiece: "he always got a point or two" out of this one! Around 1992: Sigred Axelrad, Nat and Vivian

Phyllis Trenk (Vivian's closest friend) and Vivian in June 1985 in Paris at the Air Show. The two couples travelled together on vacations every year for twenty-five years.

Top Row: Vivian, Kenneth, Daniel, Bottom Row: Deborah, Nat Cherie

Michelle and Guseppi Tarzoni on their wedding day, January 11, 2001

Vivian's and Nat's five grandsons. Standing left to right: Michael, Johnathan, Stephen; Sitting in front with Vivian: Chase and James
July 2000

Nat and Vivian in front of the Rolls Royce

Tom, my chauffeur of over 31 years with Nancy Cambria

The Model-T Ford I still own, parked next to the Rolls Royce

The atrium of Nat's office. Clockwise from upper left: "Walter" named by my grandson, Stephen. Closeup of "Walter," created by Seward Johnson, Jr. Everything is bronze: lamp, chair, rug...and Walter! Third photo (middle) is atrium once again, a bronze by Mitorai in foreground and "The Great Bear" from Doug Hyde, carved in one piece of stone. (Lower right) A closer look at the bronze by Mitorai.

Tombstone in Nat's office, which he bought around 1970

Nathan L. Serota,
taken 2001

My business cards

20

My Love, Vivian . . . and Marrying Her

Forword by Cheryl Lee Terry

"The Visionary Aquarian Sun combined with Bountiful Jupiter in ambitious Leo -- endowed Nathan with the ability to see the next horizon -- even in the darkest hour. The intense Cosmic mix of Mars and his Moon in passionate Scorpio compelled him to greet challenges and obstacles as kindling for his enthusiasm for life. But with Venus in security conscious Capricorn, he needed a strong partner and solid family base to nurture his confidence, cheer him on and give him a reason to go out and conquer his world. And when he first saw the beautiful Virgo Vivian -- he simply fell in love. And with that Scorpio Mars/Moon determination and Jupiter/Leo romantic soul he proclaimed that she would be his life partner. With the three elements Water, Fire and Air prominent in his chart, Nathan is a true lover of life, adventure and of course -- Vivian."

-*Cheryl Lee Terry,*
Astrologer/Numerologist

Vivian and I danced together many times at black-tie affairs for charity organizations, which she attended with her husband. Over time, we felt a growing and irresistible attraction toward one another. In fact, unbeknownst to me then, Vivian admitted that she'd pursued me a few times earlier, finding excuses to phone. Once, she called wanting me to build a bomb shelter in the basement of her lovely home; another time, she wanted to know if I could get tickets for one of the top Broadway shows. Don't kid yourself, a man thinks he's running after a woman, but the woman is really chasing him.

George Farkas celebrated his sixty-fifth birthday with a grand party in Paris. I booked a suite in the George V Hotel and invited Vivian to go to that romantic city for five days with me. I didn't tell my wife, but Vivian actually got approval, a written note from her husband saying she could go with me. We had a glorious time staying in a beautiful hotel, enjoying Paris and each other for five days.

After those idyllic days in Paris, I said to Vivian: "You know, if someone loves a women, they would never give them permission to spend five days in romantic Paris with another man. Your husband doesn't love you." Vivian agreed. She'd already realized her marriage was crumbling. She'd seen the women's phone numbers listed in her husband's book and had been told by others about his numerous conquests.

Rather than returning to the States right away, Vivian suggested we go on to London. This way we could both prolong having to face our spouses, but more importantly, we could prolong the glorious, romantic time we were having together. She called her husband and told him she was going to London, but he didn't ask any questions, because frankly, he was glad for the freedom.

We were falling in love--hopelessly, head over heels in love. I wanted to do something, give Vivian a fabulous gift, to show her how much I loved her. In London, I offered to buy her a white Cornish convertible. She stared up at me, her eyes full of love and belief in me. "I don't want the car. I want you," she said.

And I wanted her.

George Farkas told me I was simply trading one headache for another and advised me not to divorce my wife to marry Vivian. About that time, Vivian's husband was not being kind to her. I loved her and wanted to take care of her. I wanted to make her happy and give her a better life. Over the next months, I kept coming back to Vivian and trying to figure out a way we could be together. We met at every possible opportunity, growing more certain of our love every day. I *knew* I had found the woman I wanted, the right woman to share my life.

However, I didn't feel right about breaking up a home if it could be saved. I suggested Vivian take the children and go to a hotel and see if her husband followed her. I arranged it, and she took the three children, the youngest still an infant in diapers, to stay at the St. Moritz. From her room, she called Stewart and told him where she was. She told him she couldn't stand the way things were between them and she'd give him another chance if he came and got her. He told her to have a good time. She stayed at the hotel for three days, and he never came to get her.

Vivian's husband knew she had a boyfriend who wanted to marry her, but he didn't know it was me. Their marriage was basically over and he didn't care that his wife had a boyfriend. Because I was older and his competitor in the same business, his ego would have taken a beating had he known it was me. Stewart fancied himself quite a lover, and how would it look to all his friends in business that Nat Serota had stolen his wife? She didn't just run off with Joe Smith from around the corner. He would have to retaliate.

Concerned that Stewart would cause trouble if he knew about me, we decided to keep our love affair under wraps. Vivian refused to tell him *who* wanted to marry her. Worried her husband would follow her or have her followed, she came up with a different disguise whenever she went out to meet me. Some of them were pretty interesting. I'll never forget one night when I picked her up on Fifth Avenue in Manhattan, after she'd left her husband and was staying at the Carlyle Hotel on Madison Avenue with three kids and a maid. I sat in my car on that foggy, rainy night, excitedly waiting to meet Vivian, when along came a hunchbacked, old lady. She banged on my window, and I wished she'd go away and leave me alone. It turned out to be Vivian in disguise, complete with a pillow on her back! She disguised herself on numerous occasions and came up with some pretty creative ideas.

Vivian remembers:

"I wore a very blonde wig, and I would go into Bloomingdales wearing it, then go up the elevator or into the restroom, then zoom down the other elevator and come out looking completely different wearing a big, floppy hat or another wig. I'd stop and, from under my hat, I'd peer around to make sure no one was watching me, then walk out. Just like you see in the movies; it was very dramatic, very romantic. "

During those early days, having to go to great lengths to sneak romantic moments alone made our time together all the more precious. At one point, to get away from Stewart, Vivian took two of her children to stay with her mother in Atlantic City (the eldest was away at summer camp). Each afternoon, her mother would watch the children while Vivian ran off to meet her "romantic love" for an hour or two at the tiny local airport.

I used to run away from New York in the afternoons and fly to Atlantic City in a tiny two-seater plane just to spend a couple of hours with her. Vivian waited for me on the tarmac, and I'd wave to her from the small plane as it landed, like a scene from a Cary Grant movie. We hugged and kissed, then spent the afternoon together holding hands and talking, while the pilot waited to take me back to New York.

Vivian's husband, Stewart, was a violent man, and he went crazy when he discovered that *Serota* was the man in love with his wife. He attacked me on several occasions. The first time he tried to run me over with his car, and I managed to jump out of the way of his speeding car but fell down and hurt myself. Another night, Stewart physically attacked me while Vivian and I were walking home on a crowded New York street. Nobody would even stop to help us, and Vivian beat him with her shoe to try to make him stop pummeling me. I ended up with eight stitches over my eye.

Stewart continued to make Vivian's life difficult, and she grew increasingly afraid of him and went into hiding. One time, when she and her children were staying with her mother, Stewart came and knocked her mother down and kidnapped the children. Not knowing where they were made us frantic, although Vivian understood he wouldn't harm his children, that his actions were aimed at getting back at her. A couple of days later, she found them, and in order not to upset them, she pretended to have been away on a vacation. Another time, she went to her former residence to pack up her belongings and found the house empty--not a stick of furniture or a single thing--*he'd totally cleaned it out*. She eventually recovered some of her personal belongings through her sister-in-law. As I talk about those troubled times, which are now just memories, I am happy for all the blessed years we've had together since, and I jokingly remind Vivian that I've bought her a few houses since then.

But in the 1960s, the divorce laws were tougher, and the only way to get a divorce was by proving adultery. Vivian hired a detective to follow her husband, who had been having numerous affairs of his own for some time. She flew to Puerto Rico to get proof of Stewart's adultery so she could file for divorce. At the same time, I was under a lot of pressure from my family and decided I'd had enough, so I ran off to Florida without telling anyone in a wild attempt to escape.

Vivian recalls the story:

"I'll never forget crouching in the bushes in Puerto Rico with that detective at one o'clock in the morning waiting to crash through the door and catch my husband in bed with two women. Then I turned on the radio and heard the news: "Millionaire Disappears on the Beach." Here I was trying to get a divorce and Nat had disappeared--I didn't know what to think. All I could do was hold on to what he'd told me before he left. He'd said, "Vivian, I can't tell you what I'm going to do, but I'll be back for you. Remember, no matter what happens, I love you and I promise I'll be back for you."

Meanwhile, the news of Nat's disappearance and suspected suicide was splashed all over the papers, a police search was mounted with helicopters, and his sister even went up in the Good Year Blimp looking for a body. Here I was in Puerto Rico with a crazy husband and a detective, and now I heard nothing from Nat. I had faith in his love and what he'd told me. I believed that, whatever had happened to him, I would see him again and we'd be together forever. It was such a naive, complete and wonderful faith. I was very young, and I believed everything Nat told me. And he'd told me that he'd be back for me."

Granted, my disappearance was dramatic and perhaps a little desperate. I left my clothes and my wallet with my identification on the beach as if I'd committed suicide, just like in *A Star Is Born*. I disappeared for about a week, went off to the Keys and grew a beard. At the time, I wanted my family to think I was gone. I wanted them to get off my back and leave me alone. I wanted to make a new life with Vivian and be happy.

I called Vivian when she returned to New York. "I can't tell you where I am," I said, running a hand over the bristle on my chin, "but I'll be home in a few days." She told me she'd caught her husband and had the proof she needed to file for divorce. It seemed things were looking up for us, at least on her end.

Vivian and I were some years apart in age. I was only six years older than her mother, but that didn't matter to either of us--love doesn't discriminate. About five months after our whirlwind Paris romance, Vivian left her husband. Two years later, after the Puerto Rican stakeout, they were divorced, but Stewart refused to give her a cent, not a thing, and agreed only to a minimum amount of child support. Vivian was granted full custody of their three children, Deborah, Dena, and Daniel, and in the years that followed, she never saw a dime of that child support. She received nothing but trouble from her ex-husband.

I had moved out of the home I'd shared with Fay, but she refused to divorce me. I went to Mexico for a divorce, and en route, the plane caught fire twice. The first time, the pilot landed in Texas and the flames were put out. We took off again, only to have the plane catch fire again. I was sure it was God punishing me. The plane landed safely a second time, at another airport, and another plane was found to take us to Tijuana. What a life!

I kept trying *and trying* to file for divorce. Fay went to a sharp lawyer and had herself declared my legal wife in the state of New York, so our divorce was never legal in my home state where my property and assets were held. Nonetheless, I married Vivian in Connecticut in a legal ceremony conducted by Judge McGinty.

I was *married to two women for twenty-one years*, and that's a fact!

Naturally, Vivian was disturbed that I had another wife. I married her five times to reassure her of my continued love and devotion. The second time was in Baltimore where my sister lived. There we got married spiritually, in a Jewish ceremony at the Synagogue conducted by a Rabbi. The third time was in Tijuana, Mexico, at one of those little chapels.

Although my Mexican divorce was not recognized in the United States, I was legally divorced in the land of salsa and margaritas.

Another time, we were in Los Angeles, driving along Wilshire Boulevard, when I spotted a Spanish church with a sign advertising marriages done immediately. On the spur of the moment I turned to Vivian, "You want to get married again?"

She laughed gleefully. "Let's do it."

We were married for the fourth time by a Spanish priest in California. Our marriage was legal there because we signed the proper form which went through the state courts, although my Mexican divorce was still not recognized. So, now we'd been married by a judge, a rabbi and a priest.

In 1987, Fay finally agreed to divorce me. For the fifth and final time, Vivian and I were legally married by a judge at the municipal building on Center Street in New York City on November 9, 1987. For the first twenty-one years of our marriage we'd had a marvelous time and enjoyed every day together, joined in love and our shared life, married in both spiritual and legal ceremonies. Now that our marriage was legal in our home state, nothing changed between us; we continued to treasure every moment together.

For twenty-one years it hadn't bothered me to be married to two women. It never really changed my life, nor did repeating the ceremony with Vivian so many times. If I added all my married years together the total would be greater than my age today--as if I'd been married before I was born!

The life I continued to share with my second wife was full and loving. To this day, I look forward to coming home to Vivian every night. I truly enjoy her company and enjoy having dinner with her, whether we stay home or go out. She is a terrific, beautiful lady--my lover and my friend. We even talk on the phone three or four times every day while I'm at work.

21

Life With Vivian and the Children

Through the years, Vivian and I experienced many things together, shared heartbreaks and happiness, and supported each other through difficult times. I loved and cared for Vivian's children as if they were my own. Deborah was five years old, Dena was three, and Daniel was only a year old when I came into their lives.

Dena was a very sick girl from the day she was born. She had a severe learning disability and wore braces on her legs, from her hips to her ankles. She lived at home, under the constant care of Vivian and 'round-the-clock nurses. One year we went to Mexico for Christmas with Deborah and Daniel. We decided it wouldn't be safe for Dena to accompany us, since she wouldn't be able to get the medical care she needed in Mexico. Dena spent the holidays with her grandmother in Miami, and the two had a great time.

The rest of us stayed at the Princess Hotel in Acapulco--Vivian, myself and the two little kids, then ages four and six--our first vacation since getting married. Some of Vivian's girlfriends from Philadelphia, where she had gone to school, were coming down to join us with their families over the holidays. At that time, Vivian was newly married to a financially successful husband. She brought along several hundred thousand dollars worth of jewelry to Mexico, to wear and show off to her girlfriends.

Near the end of our stay in Acapulco, we were enjoying every minute of it when Vivian suddenly got a call from her mother in Florida. Dena was having seizures and had been taken to Mount Sinai Hospital. Of course, we got hysterical and shipped the two other kids home on a plane with friends to New York, then flew directly to Miami. When we arrived, Dena was coming along well at Mount Sinai. We stayed at Howard Johnson's near the hospital and, for the next four days, took care of Dena, along with the doctors and nurses. Just after New Year's, Dena was about to be released from hospital because she was making such good progress. I had to get back to New York for business and asked Vivian if she would be okay with Dena on her own. She agreed that I ought to go.

Before I left Florida, I stopped in to see my partner who was spending the winter there. He'd lost a few bets on the seasonal football games, as I used to, and owed a bookmaker a lot of money. He gave me $10,000 cash to take back to New York with me to pay off his debts.

I made a plane reservation and returned to the hotel to get my suitcase. I thought it would be helpful if I took all of Vivian's jewelry back with me, rather than leaving it in the safe at Howard Johnson's. While in Mexico, I'd bought about fifty gold coins. They were a popular investment at the time, and each one was worth a bundle. They weighed down my load, but I packed them too. I stopped by the hospital, with my luggage, to say good-bye before going to the airport.

I'd stuffed Vivian's jewelry into a Chivas Regal purple velvet bag, and I carried that bag, the gold coins, my partner's $10,000, and my own cash with my jacket over my arm. When I got to the hospital, I explained to Vivian what I was doing, then ran down to the gift shop to get a brown paper bag to wrap the jewelry and coins. I didn't want them to become anyone else's business when I got on the plane. I called a cab, and the driver loaded my luggage into the trunk. The airport was only three minutes away, and I asked him to wait for me outside; I paid the driver to relax in the Florida sunshine so I could have a few extra minutes with my wife.

Vivian and I sat on the sofa in the hospital rest area, talking softly and saying goodbye. Dena was in her room sleeping comfortably under the care of her nurse. Feeling the heat, I took off my jacket and folded it on the sofa and placed the package of jewelry carefully beside it. Vivian and I told each other how much we'd miss each other until the last possible minute I could leave for the airport. I kissed her goodbye, grabbed my jacket, and strode out to the cab. "I'll call you when I get to New York," I called over my shoulder as Vivian headed back to Dena's room.

I wasn't in the cab two minutes when the horrible realization of what I'd done hit me like sledge hammer. *Oh, my God, I left the f--kin' jewelry on the sofa!*

Panic setting in, I told the cab driver to turn around and get back to the hospital *fast*. He set a speed record. I ran up the stairs, taking them two at a time, to the sofa in the rest area. The package was gone!

In under eight minutes someone had found treasure--my carefully wrapped package of jewelry and gold Mexican coins. I didn't know what the hell I was going to do. I'd lost it all--Vivian's jewelry, the gold coins, the cash, my Piaget watch, and my Rolex watch, which was the first one I'd ever owned.

I called Eli Quain, a friend who owned a luggage shop on Collins Avenue in Miami, because he was one of the political boys there and I wanted his help. I asked him to call the chief of police for me and keep it confidential. I canceled my flight and stayed in Miami, hoping the authorities would catch the thief.

Eli assured me, "Okay, Nat, don't worry about it. Nobody will know.

It's nobody's business." Would you believe it? The very next morning the headline screamed across the front page of *The Miami Herald*: "Will Be a Cold Day in Hell When They Find the Jewelry." The story about my stolen package was in all the newspapers.

Dena recovered, and we all returned home to New York. The following Sunday, I was sound asleep at eight in the morning when the phone rang. A man with a heavy Spanish accent was on the other end of the line. "Sir, you are people lost jewelry at the hospital, *si*?"

"Yes," I said.

Switching to Spanish, he asked me if I understood Spanish.

I understood about that much and told him, "No, I don't speak Spanish."

In broken English he said, "*Mi amigo*, he found it. He return to you. You get someone speak Spanish, *si*? I call, one hour."

I was living at the Plaza penthouse at that time. I found the building supervisor and asked him if he had anyone on the payroll who spoke both Spanish and English. He did.

Sure enough, they called back in an hour and I had my translator ready. I was told the guy in Miami said, "This friend, he don't want to be locked up, he just wants a little reward, then he'll give back the package."

We made arrangements to fly back to Miami and pick up the package. Through my translator, I told the Spanish guy he'd recognize me at the airport because I'd wear a blue jacket and a boutonniere. Vivian decided to come with me, and we were very excited about the possibility of getting back the jewelry. The value amounted to more than $750,000, and it was not insured.

When we boarded the plane, we coincidentally ran into Sammy Mavora, my former partner's nephew. During the trip, I told Sammy what had happened. When we landed, I asked Sammy to watch out for me to make sure those guys didn't hit me over the head. Who knows who the hell I was dealing with here?

It was up to me to decide what kind of money the reward should be. When I got off the plane, the Spanish guy spotted me, and I walked toward him with Sammy following at a discrete distance. I realized at once that there was not just one guy but three Spanish guys--Cubans, I think. *And they didn't have my package.*

They explained the jewels were in a pawn shop. "I have pawn ticket," one told me in English. "I need $2,000 reward for my friend, then I give you ticket."

I knew right then they were lying. They were trying to grab me for two grand. I didn't give them a nickel! In the meantime, they were pretty sharp and spotted Sammy. "Who is that baldheaded guy back there watching us?" demanded the same man.

I didn't like the situation, *not one bit*. But I was certain they were lying, and I told them to go to hell. I managed a menacing tone when I said, "Get the hell away from me." And they turned around and left.

Vivian and I spent the rest of the day in Miami. We talked to the FBI and reported the shakedown. The stolen jewelry was never recovered. Luckily, I had paid by check for everything I lost, so I was able to deduct that loss from my income tax over the years. I had no insurance on the valuables and, despite this experience, I still don't. In time, I replaced all of Vivian's jewelry.

When I reported to my partner how I'd lost his money and offered to replace his $10,000, he refused to accept it. He shrugged and said, "I lost another ten, that's all. Forget it."

Sadly, we lost Dena at age sixteen. She became ill and died suddenly in Atlantic City, where Vivian had taken our three children to visit their grandmother, accompanied by Dena's nurse. Our grief was too terrible, *heart wrenching*. But I want Vivian to tell you . . . .

"When our daughter, Dena, died Nat took care of all the expenses and emotionally upheld the whole family. He flew to Atlantic City immediately when I called to tell him. Nat managed to handle the arrangements and be there for me at the same time he was dealing with his own grief. When we walked into the funeral parlor, I saw Nat beside Dena's coffin, stroking her hair. My two children were brave and wonderful; we all held hands. Daniel had been in the room with me and tried to revive Dena.

We are a close family, and sharing our grief brought us even closer. We all cried together. Deborah and Daniel used to take turns at night listening for her seizures through the special door we'd made into Dena's room. For all of us, the reality of dealing with the overwhelming loss--that we'd never see her again, never hold her hand again--was tremendously difficult to bear. They say the loss of a child is unbearable grief, the deepest, never-ending pain, and I believe that is true."

However, this tragic experience didn't seem to soften up Vivian's first husband, Dena's biological father. When Dena's body was brought to the funeral parlor, Stewart stopped Vivian on her way in to see her daughter. It is Jewish tradition, for a family to pray and mourn together, to sit Shiva for a dead relative. Stewart insisted Vivian sit down with his parents, but added that he wanted to speak to her in front of Dena before she sat with his family. As hard as it was to walk into the funeral parlor to view her daughter, Vivian agreed, and the two went in to pay their respects together. Standing there, Stewart apologized to Vivian for not being a good father, for not wanting to see his daughter when she was alive because she was retarded, and for not paying any of her medical bills. Vivian remembers more about those hard times:

". . . It really destroyed me, but somehow we got through it. When

you are depressed, you literally can't get out of bed unless somebody actually comes and takes you out. I had a very loyal group of girlfriends who came over to get me out of bed every morning. They took me to dance lessons and exercise classes.

When somebody close to you dies, you feel guilty. I dwelled on guilty thoughts, on what ifs, on what I should have done differently to prevent Dena's death. I should have gotten her to the hospital sooner; I should have called the ambulance earlier; I should have, I should have . . . . The first year following a death is spent writhing in horrible guilt.

I went to a psychologist for help. Through therapy and time, I came to understand that Dena's death was out of my control. It was her time to go. I came to believe that God had been good to our little girl, and to us, to take her so quickly at that moment in time. She had a kind, gentle nature, but Dena was just beginning to understand that she couldn't do what other children could, that she never would be able to. That knowledge frustrated her, and she suffered. I learned to accept that God had chosen the time and place of my daughter's passing and had taken her before she would have had to be put into a home. Nat endured the pain with us."

Vivian and I experienced other tough times during our married life, and we always helped each other get through them. Early on, Vivian's ex-husband had created almost insurmountable problems for her. He provided no child support and didn't always show up for his visits with his children. He and Vivian often fought about the kids.

One day, after yet another fight regarding the children, Stewart again came after me physically. He showed up at my office building around five-thirty, barged through the glass door at reception and straight into my office. We got into a fist fight, and he broke my jaw. I didn't know at the time that he'd had a fight with Vivian and was picking on me to get back at her. I also didn't know I had a broken jaw until about a week later when I went to see the doctor because the pain was getting to be too much. My jaw was wired shut for several weeks, and the only good thing about that was that I lost some weight.

Some years later, when we were married and living on 85th Street and Park Avenue, I went downstairs to get my car out of the garage. A door from the lobby led to a vestibule where there was another door which opened to the garage. Stewart was waiting for me there and physically attacked me again. That time, I filed an assault complaint and took him to court, but the judge threw out the case. Stewart said I'd stolen his wife from him, and the judge didn't want to get involved.

In the poor economy of the seventies, Stewart had some difficult times and lost the supermarkets he owned. One morning in the mid-eighties, I got a call from one of my supermarket contacts, Mel Weiss, who told us Stewart had been killed. Vivian remembers:

"Nat was a saint to all of us by opening our home to the members of Stewart's family for seven days to sit Shiva. This shows how generous Nat has been, because he certainly could have said he didn't want those people in his home."

We did it for Deborah and Daniel, which is the way it should be. We then took the two children away to Europe for the summer. By that time, we all needed a vacation; it was precious time to get away and relax.

22

Economic Hard Times

1977 was a tough year for us. The real estate market was on the fritz, and we had to move out of our beautiful penthouse and into a smaller apartment in New York, jamming all our furniture in. But none of that was important after Dena died. The important thing was that we were together as a family, a team, helping each other through our grief and healing.

At one point in the 1970s, I nearly lost all my money. The real estate business suffered during this period when interest rates were sky high; new business was practically nonexistent, and cash flow became very tight. Fortunately, I didn't lose my property, but things were not good financially for me or any other builder at this time. However, we managed to live through it. Many others did not.

I attribute this largely to my positive attitude, my tenacity, and Vivian's loving support. For several years, things were bad--no question about it--but I remained positive. I always believed that tomorrow was going to be a better day. Every day I encountered tough situations I had to deal with, and every day I'd put the problems behind me. I had the ability to detach at the day's end, to detach from each problem and charge on toward the next day, fully expecting it to be better. I think it's true that every cloud has a silver lining. Yes, everything seemed to be going against me, but tomorrow was another day--the clouds would disappear and the sun would shine again. My policy is to live every day to the fullest and believe tomorrow will be better than today.

I was forty-nine when I married Vivian. At the time, I was still legally married to Fay in name only. My first wife had hired a hot shot New York City lawyer and threatened to ruin us. My lawyer advised me not to live in New York State with Vivian and the kids, but rather to move to New Jersey.

In 1969, we moved into Horizon House, a big apartment complex on the river front in New Jersey, directly overlooking New York City. It included several buildings and more than eighteen hundred units. I ended up becoming the leader of the tenants' association after I discovered that a well-known New York restaurant had made a deal to open a location in the North Tower of Horizon House, our building. Like many of the tenants, I objected to living with a restaurant right in the lobby of our building.

I was busy working on other building projects and suggested to Vivian that she bring the issue to the mayor's attention. "Find out how they can possibly put a restaurant in our lobby when it's not zoned for a restaurant."

Vivian went to see the mayor, along with three other women residing at Horizon House. She asked the mayor why and how he had made the zoning change, and how a restaurant could possibly open in the North Tower without the approval of the tenants' association.

Mayor Licata wouldn't even listen to their concerns; instead he embarrassed them. "What are you ladies doing here? Why aren't you home cooking?" he asked. Vivian and her friends stomped out of his office, fighting mad.

That night, when Vivian told me what the mayor had said to them, I vowed to start a war. I created a tenants' association, representing over a thousand tenants in the complex, by inviting about twenty people to our apartment. Suddenly, I had become the leader of a tenant army and now found myself chairman of the board of Horizon House. The mayor had insulted four of our residents, including my wife, and I was determined to fight him. With an election right around the corner, I gathered my forces.

Burt Ross was a tenant in our building, and he wanted to run for mayor. He came to see me. His father lived in New York City and had made a lot of money in the stock market; he had money behind him. Ross launched a campaign for mayor, and I backed him. Vivian organized all the women in the building to put up circulars, along with help from the children after school. Burt Ross became mayor. The restaurant never opened. Everyone was happy.

At the same time, I became spokesperson for the board of a new building called The Plaza which sat high on a cliff in New Jersey. I'd purchased a spacious condominium there, but it wasn't ready yet. My new penthouse apartment took up the whole top floor of the building, seventy-two hundred square feet, and featured a stunning view of Bear Mountain, Central Park, the river, and every bridge going south.

While I waited for the new apartment to be ready, I had trouble renewing my lease on the Horizon House apartment and literally was forced to move out in the middle of the night. The owners wouldn't renew or extend my lease because I'd instigated the fight with the tenants' association. They actually got the sheriff and physically threw us out. We moved all night with three moving vans into, what was then, a very unfinished apartment in the Plaza. But despite its chaotic state, Vivian and I loved the new place. and we couldn't wait to settle in.

My wife always stood by me, *for richer, or poorer . . . .*

There was one particularly bad time around 1974-75, when Vivian went back to Jerry Blickman, who owned Blickman Jewelry, to sell all her jewelry. He was a true gentleman. Not only did he give Vivian back the money paid for the jewelry, he wrote her the check on the spot. His daughter, Michelle Blickman, has been a very good friend to me over the past twenty-five years also. I met her when I had business dealings with her father--she was just learning the business at the time. Soon after we met, her father passed away. She had taken over for her dad and proved to be an honorable wheeler-dealer. She has been one of those rare women who knows how to listen, deal, and talk to especially difficult men like me. I adore Michelle. (Incidentally, two years ago Michelle met Guiseppe Torroni, a uniquely caring man, and within a year they were married.)

We had only been married about five years then, and I had taken on the responsibility of caring for three young children from her previous marriage. I now had two households to support, because I also had to take care of Fay and my two sons. I had five kids and two wives to keep alive, well, and happy. And unfortunately, it was a time when I was running terribly short of money.

This poor economic time coincided with the breakup of my partnership with Elias. The banks were none too eager to lend me any money. Everything that could go wrong did, and I was really having a tough time of it. At this time, my partner and I began our long court battle, and he was giving me a rough time and no financial help. I had no cash flow and huge legal bills. Everything was tumbling downhill.

One of the gifts I'd given Vivian early on in our courtship was a very special necklace made of coins which had belonged to Abigail Adams, President Adams' wife. I hated to sell it, but I had to. This was sometime later, and I was desperate for cash. Michelle gave me the same amount I had paid for it. It wound up being sold at auction two years later for a million dollars. Finally, the economic wheel turned, and my building business began thriving. I regret that even when my fortunes changed, I never retrieved that historic necklace for Vivian.

The wheel always turns and you have to have spirit and know that if you work at it, you will be a winner. That said, I think one day the economy is going to fall on its ass. It will take people with this kind of strength of spirit to make it through. I sincerely believe my positive philosophy is what made me successful. I tell my children and grandchildren, "You can get it, anything you want. Believe in yourself! Make up your damn mind *you can do it*."

23

Fighting the "Boys"

When Burt Ross first became mayor, he offered me a position on the board. I suggested, since I was a developer, I'd be most qualified to sit on the city planning board, but he didn't have an opening there. Instead, I became the commissioner of the parking authority. I didn't have to do much except record some parking meters, but I was now a member of Fort Lee's politico.

Eight months after the election, I heard about land being bought up by Arthur Sutton (a builder I knew) for a proposed project on the edge of the Hudson River near the George Washington Bridge. I discovered he intended to build a huge commercial project practically in my back yard, to develop fourteen acres right next to The Plaza where we now lived in our fabulous penthouse.

These developers had to apply to the town for numerous variances and zoning changes--fifteen variances to allow them to build millions of square feet of office buildings, apartments, movie theaters, health spas, and retail outlets. The George Washington Bridge, which our home overlooked, provided access from New York to Fort Lee, New Jersey, a town of 30,000 people, and as it was, the traffic was insane. I had to get on that bridge every day to go to my office on Long Island, already a hellish commute of about an hour and twenty minutes. This was the last straw--developers wanted to block off my building and bring even more people into the area.

Determined not to permit the zoning changes they needed, I hired a couple of lawyers, at a cost of $30,000, to fight them in court. I suspected who was behind the project, but that didn't scare me. Connected or not, these developers were doing something I didn't like, and I was going to fight them. I brought in my crew of lawyers, and we all showed up in court twice a week for three or four months for the zoning hearings.

As the fight began to heat up, I got a phone call at home from Joe Valentine, owner of Valentine Electric, a big company that handled the electrical work for our buildings. I had never met Valentine in person, but I certainly knew who he was. The man had a lot of pull in New Jersey.

He began, "Mr. Serota . . . ."

"Mr. Valentine," I said, "you did a lot of good work in my apartment. I sent you plenty of money, remember?"

"I didn't call about money. I want to talk to you about something else. Saturday. Can I see ya then?"

Curious, I made an appointment with him to come to my apartment. The apartment was now completely finished and elaborately decorated; it was *fantastic*, and we loved it. It had its own elevator which went directly up to the penthouse. Saturday morning, the doors slid open and Joe Valentine stepped off. He was a short, stocky guy, looking for all the world like "Little Caesar." I invited him to sit down and asked what I could do for him.

"I don't think you realize what you're doing, Mr. Serota," he said. "You've got all these people up in arms. You're leading a fight which will hurt them. You're putting thousands of people out of work and I just don't think you realize what you're doing."

"So what? I live here," I said.

He leaned forward. "We *strongly* object. Me and my partner, Mr. De Arco."

I knew that name, and I realized exactly what was going on here. Valentine was connected. Now, as long as nobody got hurt, I had no real objection. What do I care what these guys do? But right this minute, one of the boys was sitting in my living room, threatening me to get me to back down from my zoning fight.

I looked him squarely in the eyes. "Mr. Valentine, are you threatening me?"

"No, no . . . I'm not threatening you."

"Yeah, you are. Let me explain something to you. I'm fifty-two years old, and I've had guys like you bullshit me for years. I'm not taking any more of your nonsense. Get the f--k out of my apartment!"

The man left. I was nervous because these were tough guys, so I thought I'd better go to see my attorney. George Soll (now deceased) was one of the top lawyers in New York at the time, and I needed his advice about my situation. I went to his office and explained what was happening, told him what I knew about Arthur Sutton's plans and Investors Funding, the financial group behind his project. I wanted Soll to check them out, get a detective on them.

"The "boys" are getting in on it," I said. "What should I do?"

My attorney said that since Fay had accepted Vivian and I were together, and she wasn't likely to make trouble for us now, Vivian and I should move back to New York as husband and wife. In fact, he strongly suggested that we move out of New Jersey. *Immediately.* I didn't want to move. We'd just fixed up the penthouse and it had cost a fortune, so I told him I'd think about it. He warned me not to think too long.

The next day I got a phone call at my office from De Arco. I'd thrown his partner out of my apartment on Saturday, and now *he* wanted to see me. "I have a plan for ya," he said.

"What!"

"Please, Mr. Serota, don't be rough. I want to be nice about this. I just want to see you because I have a plan where we can both win."

I wanted to get the hell away because I was afraid of these guys. Instead, I found myself agreeing to meet with De Arco the following Saturday.

"Forget what you said to my partner last week. Let me ask you a question, Serota," Joe De Arco said when we met. "If you didn't live here, would you care what happened to these fourteen acres?"

"No," I answered truthfully.

"So give me a price for your apartment, and I'll buy you out. You can live here for six months until you find somewhere else. Then move out and *get off this case.*"

After he left, I anxiously called my attorney, and George gave me sound advice. He told me to give them a price and, if they bought it, take the money and run. Get the hell out!

Okay, I could see the wisdom of getting out. Naturally, I wanted to make a little profit, so I priced the apartment at a million dollars. They wouldn't go for it. After some negotiating, they agreed to pay me $900,000. Listing themselves as Investors Funding, they put up $215,000 cash as a deposit, and my lawyer held it in escrow.

Realizing I wouldn't take any more of their bullshit, Investors Funding lowered the scope of their development project so we would both come out of it looking good. Instead of building three million square feet, they did away with the part I'd objected to and proposed to build a little over two million, as long as I'd back down from the zoning battle and the board could pass it. They worked with me, and I made the deal. Everything was fine until the mayor got nervous, and in the end, the project was never built.

Things have a way of catching up with people. One week after we'd signed the paperwork on the apartment sale and my attorney had put the money in escrow, De Arco and Valentine were picked up by the FBI for passing $100,000 to the mayor.

Earlier, during the zoning fight, the mayor had called me and tried to talk me into backing off. He'd gone on and on about what a good project it was (which it wasn't), and that made me suspect the mayor might be involved. Apparently, he got nervous about the situation, and went to the U. S. Attorney. Without admitting his own involvement, he plotted to set up De Arco and Valentine. Because of the mayor's help, the FBI blocked off a restaurant on the edge of Fort Lee on the Sunday morning when the payoff was to take place, and they caught De Arco and Valentine red-handed with the bribe.

24

Grand Jury, the Trial and Appeal

I usually went away to the French Riviera every summer, and the summer of 1975 was no different. While I was in France, my office got a call from the government prosecutor for Newark, New Jersey, asking to see me. I wondered why.

When I went to see the U.S. Attorney, he brought in another attorney--they always bring in *another attorney*--and they asked me to tell them what I'd had to do with Valentine and De Arco. I had nothing to hide, so I told them the story, exactly the truth. They wanted me to repeat it for the Grand Jury, to involve me in their case to indict the mayor, De Arco, and Valentine. On the advice of my lawyer, who concurred that I had done *nothing illegal*, I appeared before the Grand Jury.

It was the biggest mistake in the world. The Grand Jury was not twelve men and women like a court jury, but rather twenty-five or more. They sat in something like a small theater audience and listened while the U.S. Attorney asked me questions. Long before his grilling was over, I could see the direction of the questions he was posing. He was trying to put the finger on me, trying to make himself look good in front of the press at my expense.

"Are you trying to make me the fool or the devil here? Did I do something wrong?" I asked. I did not get an answer--only more questions. I felt like I was being roasted on a spit. When the prosecutor had first called me, I'd gone directly to my attorney, George Soll, who had, in turn, met with him on my behalf. Soll knew the whole story of what had happened between Investors Funding, whose name appeared on the contract as the buyer of the penthouse, and me. He had represented me in my fight against the zoning change for the development and the subsequent sale of my apartment to them. He knew I had absolutely nothing to do with developing this project, nor had I anything to do with the attempt to bribe the mayor.

The U.S. Attorney asked Soll to put my statement of innocence in writing. My lawyer left his office, promising to have my statement prepared and delivered to him in two days, and the prosecutor agreed to wait until he received the papers before taking any further action. As Soll drove across the George Washington Bridge, back to New York from the New Jersey office, he flipped on the car radio. A news broadcast announced that five men, including Nat Serota, had been indicted. Soll pounded his fist on the steering wheel. *That son-of-a-bitch hadn't said a word to him.* He'd sat across the desk wearing a poker face, talking about paperwork and waiting, all the while knowing he'd just gone public with my indictment.

I should have known then that somebody was out to get me. But *I knew I was innocent*, and I believed in the system. The next day, the story of my indictment blazed across the pages of the *New York Times*. Naturally, I was disturbed about being indicted. This had never happened to me before.

I appeared in front of a judge who set my bail at $100,000. Each of the five people indicted in this case had the same figure set as bail. I didn't have to put up the whole amount, only ten percent, so I wrote out a check for $10,000.

The case didn't come up for four or five months. In the meantime, all the publicity about my indictment seriously disturbed my credit rating. I hired Martin London of the Paul Weiss Rifkin law firm to represent me. He was a powerful attorney, a tall, good-looking guy with an impressive client list including Jackie Kennedy and Spiro Agnew during the time Agnew had been vice president.

We were all tried together: Valentine, De Arco, myself, and two others--Norman Danska and Stephen Haymes. All were in the real estate business, nice gentlemen, not connected, who had tied up with Valentine and De Arco simply because they had political pull. We were all indicted. The first time I met all of them was when we first appeared at the arraignment.

Most days during our trial, the whole group of us with our lawyers would eat lunch together. De Arco was represented by his brother; Alan Dershowitz, a famous Harvard University law professor and author, represented one of the others; Martin London represented me. We were quite the diverse group, unlikely to have lunched together under normal circumstances.

One day at lunch, De Arco implied that if this whole thing hadn't happened, they were ready to put drugs in my car and have me arrested and ruined as Chairman of the Board of Daytop Village. During the trial, it came out that if I hadn't backed down from my court case, it was rumored that someone had hired two hit men from Cleveland to see to my demise. That whole scheme broke apart when the mayor got scared and went to the FBI, who then caught the boys red-handed turning over the bribe money. Ironically, now we were all codefendants, having lunch together during our trial.

We spent twenty-six days, including Saturdays, on trial in the Newark, New Jersey courtroom in front of "hanging judge" Judge Lacey.

He was a nasty son-of- a-bitch who didn't like me at all. The jury, brought in from Tom's River, New Jersey, was sequestered for the twenty-six days, and by the end of the trial, they delivered a guilty verdict for all five of the defendants in the case. Everybody was found guilty. Period. Everybody was sentenced to five years, including me. Naturally, we all appealed.

The judge really hated me. He felt the motive of the others charged in this case was money, and he was most annoyed with me because he thought I already had more than enough money. When Judge Lacey sentenced me, he said, "You, Serota, shouldn't be here. You have money and nothing to do with these fellahs. If I could I'd give you ten years!"

I laughed, right in the judge's face, and as I sat down, my lawyer, Martin London, leaned over and asked, "Nat, what did you laugh at him for?"

"Marty, I'm not going anywhere, so forget about him."

That night, we invited all my best friends to join me at the Rainbow Room for a marvelous party. I didn't want to think about the reality of going to jail for five years, nor did I want my family and friends to dwell on it. We celebrated and laughed about Serota getting a five-year sentence as if it were just a joke the judge had told entirely for our entertainment. We had a damned good time. Nobody has ever forgotten about that party.

At this point, because of the pending appeal, I was not locked up. I was out on bail again, and paperwork was done to transfer the ten percent I'd put up before into the new bail--the same amount of $100,000. But the money never got transferred. Instead, a week and a half later I received a $10,000 check in the mail, the refund for my previous bail post. They'd made a mistake. I never told my lawyer that they'd returned my money in error. I put the check in my desk drawer, then took it out ten days later. "Oh, f--k 'em I'll cash it!" I said to myself.

I cashed the check and nobody ever knew until about a year later when my appeal was heard in the Third Circuit Supreme Court of Appeals in Philadelphia. There, the case was thrown out of court. When they analyzed my trial, they didn't believe I'd had anything to do with the charges I'd been accused of. They determined I was innocent, canceled my five-year sentence, and made a public statement to that effect.

De Arco wound up doing five years in prison. The others did maybe six months.

Martin London was a brilliant lawyer with an excellent legal team--Max Gitter, Marvin Wexler and his wife, Joan Silverman--who all worked 'round-the-clock along with him. I'll never forget them. Over the course of the trial and appeal, Marty and I became friends. He called me a week after it was all over, very happy with the results. After raving about the success of the appeal, he said, "You know, Nat, I forgot to apply to get your bail money back."

When I told him not to bother applying for it, he argued, saying I was entitled to my money. I had to admit I'd received the check already and cashed it. He went crazy. "My God, they could have hung you!"

"Yeah. It was my money," I said. We laughed about it then.

25

You Never Know Who Your Friends Are

The months after I'd been convicted (awaiting appeal) coincided with the time my partner decided he wanted to retire. Basically, I was now building on my own. The news of my conviction made all the papers (I still have most of the articles), and it didn't help my business one bit. One of the toughest things that ever happened to me was when I went to my banker to borrow $400,000 for the first time on my own to start the Shirley Shopping Center. After all, taking out a mortgage is common practice for a builder. Although the bank claimed I didn't actually have a problem, they refused me credit and suggested my partner should sign for the money.

Fine, I thought, disturbed by the banker's attitude. I went to discuss the idea with Ike. I explained that, although we were no longer partners, I needed him to sign for the loan which I would pay back within a few months. In between, I'd sign one of our buildings totally over to him as collateral to cover his loss in case I should drop dead.

He turned me down! We had been partners for twenty-five years, even after I had been the major partner, the one who had done all the work and made everything go. It bothered me deeply when Ike said he'd rather use his money to build with his son. I left his office hurt and angry.

Carl Manis, a mutual friend of ours, called me less than half an hour after Ike had turned me down. A textile manufacturer, Carl was a very good businessman who looked like Burt Lancaster. Carl asked to see me the following morning at his Manhattan office, twenty minutes away from where I was then living. I said I was too busy to come and he insisted I *must* stop by for just five minutes. I relented.

When I got there, Carl told me Ike had called him saying that I had asked him to sign for a few hundred thousand dollars and he wasn't going to give it to me. I jumped up from my chair. "What! When you called and asked me to meet you this morning, I'd just seen the son-of-a-bitch only twenty minutes before."

"Don't get excited," said Carl. He slid open his desk drawer and pulled out a big brown envelope. "Take this to the banker, and tell those bastards to give you the money."

The envelope contained a million dollars worth of negotiable U.S. bonds to cover my loan. Now, that's a good friend!

I can tell this story now, as Carl wouldn't mind. He died five or six years ago and is most certainly in Heaven. I miss him all the time, but keep him alive by telling Carl Manis stories. This story is important because it proves you never know who your true friends are going to be.

When I was arraigned for trial, I found out just how many *real friends* I had. A couple of former girlfriends called to ask if I needed money or if there was anything they could do. My true friends believed in me, trusted me, and no matter what, were there to help. I returned Carl's loan six months later

My two older sons, at this time, were in their twenties. Charles worked for me then, and he went in to sign for the loan. Even after my appeal, the bank still wanted my sons, Charles and Geoffrey, to sign for all our business loans. Daniel was in high school and couldn't have anything to do with it. He would come to work with me later at *Nathan L. Serota and Sons*.

As a general rule, I'm wary and none too fond of bankers. I've only met a half dozen over the years who I thought were extremely bright. My advice is to be aware that bankers are working for the bank, not for the customer.

In my experience, contractors can be as frustrating as bankers. For instance, the contract for the steel needed for a particular building might be a million and a half dollars. Each time I'd negotiate with the steel contractor and fight to keep the price down. After I'd give him the job, we'd shake hands on the deal we'd made. A handshake was good then; we didn't make written contracts. To keep everything straight, I'd then call my terrific bookkeeper, Terri Ragan, who has been with me for eighteen years, and instruct her to mark down that I'd agreed to pay so and so contractor a million and a half "with no extras," or whatever the deal was.

It was better to agree to a set price up front which included any changes, so both parties knew what they were getting into. Saying "no extras" was a bit of joke. There are always extras and changes in any business contract, whether the car business, cement or painting. Whatever your initial agreement or contract states, there are bound to be changes whenever the end customer or tenant buys or rents the product and wants to do something different.

Early on, I discovered that whenever I beat a contractor's brains out dollar-wise on the original contract, most of them found a way to screw me when it came to the extras at the end. By that time, I couldn't get another contractor to do the job, so I was forced to pay them close to what they wanted. For instance, if I had an air conditioning man putting in some ductwork, then I rented 50,000 square feet with twenty offices, various changes would suddenly have to be made midstream. Since those changes were not in the original air conditioning contract, the contractor would try to give me the shaft by charging a higher price for that work.

I learned how best to handle deals with contractors. My policy was always "no extras" in the initial deal, but we both knew *there would be extras*. I have never screwed a contractor for even a nickel. Many builder/developers try to beat the devil out of the contractor when it comes to paying the final payment. I don't do that. I make a deal with them in the beginning, clearly stating the dollar amount and no extras. When the job is done, I pay them the full amount agreed upon. Most of my contractors have been working with me for the past twenty to thirty years on a handshake. I stand by my handshake.

And for the contractors and tenants and all the other people I had business dealings with over the years, I leave you with these words of wisdom that some of you may have heard me say before: If I die, make sure the contractors get paid.

26

Health Interests

Introduction by friends, Arnold and Anne Kopelson:

One day, when I was exercising at the Pritikin Institute, a very attractive woman stepped onto the treadmill next to me. What was unusual about this woman was her intoxicating perfume and the numerous bracelets and rings adorning her wrists and fingers, which were not customary accessories for workout attire.

I had found that the easiest way to pass the time during an exercise period was to engage in sexual fantasy. I began a casual discussion with the woman on the treadmill, and in no time at all, my mind had conjured up an extraordinary fantasy centered around her rings and bracelets. It was abruptly interrupted by a loud, demanding voice calling, "Vivian . . . what are you doing?"

I turned to see a man with gray hair and a large diamond in his ear, descending on the two of us. Certain the man was a mobster, I imagined I was in serious trouble for talking to his girlfriend, never mind what I'd been doing in my mind.

Vivian introduced us. "Say hello to Arnold," she told the mobster.

"He's a Hollywood producer."

"What do you produce, sex films?" Nat Serota asked gruffly.

For a fleeting moment my fantasy resumed, but I laughed it off, a little nervously. "Oh sure, I'm producing a sex film right here on this treadmill, and your girlfriend is the star."

That night, Nat and Vivian had dinner with my wife, Anne, and me at the old Spago, off Sunset Boulevard in Los Angeles. I quickly learned that he was not a mobster, and was, in fact, a successful real estate developer. His girlfriend was, in fact, his wife of many years. And his gruff exterior didn't hold up for long as he got tears in his eyes when telling racy stories about his youthful days working for the railroad.

This was the beginning of our growing friendship with these two wonderful people, now in it's twelfth year. But make no mistake. Nat Serota has some strange ideas.

The first time we traveled together, we were shocked to discover this extremely wealthy man would not fly First Class. "I'm not giving my hard-earned money to those bastards. Get in the back of the plane, Vivian," Nat instructed as we were boarding. Anne and I berated him for being so cheap and punishing Vivian in this way, but he said we were crazy to waste money.

The next time we flew together, Nat bought three seats, which I thought was odd, and again told his wife to get in the back of the plane. "F--k 'em," he said in his usual eloquent fashion, "I'm not paying for First Class seats. And my three seats are more comfortable than your two anyway." When we were served our meal, Anne and I took food back to Vivian but wouldn't give any to Nat. That did it! From then on, Nat and Vivian flew First Class.

Nat Serota is one of the sweetest, warmest, most lovable men we know. Don't let his screaming fool you; he's just a big pussycat.

Arnold Kopelson

I have infinite respect for Ann and Arnold Kopelson as a working team. Arnold is an Oscar-winning producer. His partner, co-producer, and wife, Ann, is equally talented. Together, the two make an unbeatable pair, and they're inspirational in how they've managed to combine their working relationship with a loving marriage.

But, in my life, they're more than just a famous couple. While Vivian and I were at the Pritikin Institute, I suffered a heart attack. At that time, we were new friends of the Kopelsons. Vivian trusted their medical savvy, and Ann and Arnold came to my rescue. As the ambulance was arriving, Vivian, in desperation, woke the Kopelsons at 4:00 in the morning for help. Arnold told Vivian to take me to Cedar Sinai to his own doctor, Dr. Jay Schapira, who would be waiting for me when I got there. He was waiting. A brilliant doctor, he saved my life.

Ann and Arnold visited me every day in the hospital and welcomed Vivian into their home until I was released. After that, they opened their hearts even further, insisting that we both stay with them as their guests until I felt well enough to travel home. They are giving and gracious and all-round wonderful people, and I love them both dearly. I'm grateful that they are in my life.

But that doesn't explain how I started going to the Pritikin Institute.

In 1969, when Vivian told her mother she wanted to marry an older man, her mother suggested my health ought to be checked out before the wedding. As her mother put it, "there is no sense in getting married to a man if he is going to die on you." Vivian didn't explain why she wanted me to be examined by a particular doctor she knew, but I was so in love with her, I didn't question her request. I simply accompanied her to see Dr. Wolf. He was a famous doctor in New York who took care of only well-educated, well-known, and wealthy people--in my mind, a quack.

Dr. Wolf saw only select patients in an antiquated office full of all kinds of odd instruments, in his town house on the corner of 79th Street and Park Avenue. When we walked into his office, somehow I managed to refrain from comment. I almost got hysterical looking at him. A little man, about five foot three and skinny as a rail, he was wearing a white silk suit at least twenty years out of date. I was forty-nine and he had to be at least eighty!

The doctor examined me, checked my ears and eyes, and had me stick out my tongue. He took blood, urine, and performed several tests. The whole examination seemed ridiculous to me, and I couldn't believe Vivian had paid the man $265 for it. At one point, when he left the office, I said to her, "Where did you find this guy? I've never seen a doctor like this in my life!" She assured me that Dr. Wolf had a terrific reputation and insisted he was not the crook I thought he was. It didn't matter, as I was quite willing to do whatever Vivian wanted.

The following week, we returned to the cluttered office for the test results, and the doctor said everything checked out okay. Then, out of the blue, he asked me if I had any problems sleeping. I'm not sure how he knew, but I don't sleep well, never have; even today, I don't sleep more than three or four hours a night. "Don't bother counting sheep," Dr. Wolf said, "everybody does that and it doesn't work. Close your eyes and think of something pleasant, something wonderful, instead."

It dawned on me that he wanted me to close my eyes and try to sleep right there in his office. *He had to be kidding*, but I humored the old man. "What do you call pleasant?"

"Think of making love," he said.

That threw me a little. I decided I'd had enough of this quack and left.

I thought Dr. Wolf was nuts, but it turned out he wasn't nuts. His wife died a short time after I saw him, and the doctor, who had to have been eighty-five by then, promptly married his young nurse. He had his

Central Park apartment completely redecorated, put in a huge round bed and began an energetic new life with his bride.

In good health, I married Vivian, and we later shared a laugh about Dr. Wolf.

My wife was very health conscious, and three or four years after our marriage, we got involved with Nathan Pritikin. In her quest to save the life of her daughter, Vivian took it upon herself to learn everything she could about health by seeking out doctors all over the world. When she discovered she had a retarded child, she had the courage to go to places where she could find out information on what she could do.

Vivian believes you must seek out professional people and never be afraid to ask questions. Through her search for medical help and knowledge, she met Patrick McGrady, a writer who studied health topics and wrote books about them. Patrick became a good friend to both of us. When Vivian expressed concern about my diet because I was working very hard and not eating properly, Patrick suggested we go to California to see Nathan Pritikin, whom he touted as a brilliant nutritionist.

Patrick McGrady accompanied us to Pritikin's Institute in Santa Barbara and introduced us to the man who would make a big difference in my life. Pritikin had worked with Harvey Radio and claimed over a hundred inventions when, at forty-two, he suffered a heart attack. That was his wake-up call. In an effort to discover how this could have happened to the perfectly healthy man of forty-two he'd thought himself to be, he gave up inventing things to study nutrition. As a nutritionist, he became the first to advise the American Medical Association on what to eat and what not to eat; he suggested people could save themselves from heart attacks and other diseases through proper nutrition and exercise.

I became friends with Nathan Pritikin. He was a very good person and a perfect gentleman whom I genuinely admire, although he was the world's worst businessman. Every year for the past twenty-five years, I've taken two weeks off to go to the Pritikin Institute and attend his program through which people are instructed about nutrition. My association with Pritikin and the Institute has affected my life and my health greatly. The first program I attended for thirty days was at the old Pritikin Institute in a beat up hotel he'd bought and converted. The whole time I wished I had enough money to help him fix the place up. During those thirty days, I became intrigued with Nathan Pritikin, his knowledge, his philosophy and how his mind worked.

Pritikin gave me a lot to think about. He explained the reason people get heart attacks and strokes is because their arteries become clogged when they don't eat properly. My father had died of a stroke, and my mother had succumbed to a heart attack. This gave me pause.

As I mentioned, my mother was the greatest cook in America, but she didn't know much about nutrition. Nobody did in those days. As I mentioned before, we had beef at least four nights a week, lots of eggs, and sweet, heavy cream on our cereal every morning before we went to school. At that time, serving this type of food was thought to be a part of living well--the more fat you consumed, the better you ate. My mother would raise hell with the milk company if, when she checked the five bottles of milk they delivered, she discovered each did not have a thick layer of cream on top. Today we drink milk with no fat in it.

Pritikin was a forerunner of the movement to study nutrition and its effect on our health. At the Institute, there was a gym, and he instructed us about the importance of exercise, as well as the importance of making nutritious dietary choices. The food served at the Institute had no animal fats and, therefore, little cholesterol. I still don't eat egg yolks, and it is on a very rare occasion that I ever have a steak or hamburger. I mainly eat chicken with all the skin and fat trimmed off, and lots of fish.

I have learned that the basic trick to good health is regular exercise and a proper diet. Up until four years ago, my choice exercise was jogging.

I jogged four days a week, running three or four miles in Central Park on the track around the reservoir. That place is packed from six o'clock in the morning on, and I joined the throng of early morning runners, then walked two blocks home to shower and eat a healthy breakfast before heading to work. That is how Pritikin taught me to live and I credit that regime with my being alive today, now at eighty-one years old.

27

Involvement With Daytop Village

Daytop Village is one of the largest, most successful drug rehabilitation programs in the world. I first became aware of Daytop in 1975. Very impressed with the program, Vivian and I both decided to take part in it and see how we could help. We got involved by going to meetings and interacting with people to find out what was needed. At one meeting, we met the president of Daytop, Monsignor William O'Brien, who is a fantastic man and still a friend today, and we also met Brian Madden, his right-hand man.

At that time, Daytop Village operated three rehabilitation centers in upstate New York. Boys and girls with drug problems went to the centers and entered a twenty-four hour program to get the help they needed to ultimately graduate from the program drug-free. Sadly, there were more kids needing to enter the program than there were rooms to accommodate them. Daytop wanted to raise $100,000 to expand the center in Millbrook, and the federal government offered to match the $100,000 if they could raise it. I wanted to help them, but I didn't think I had the cash personally to give them. Builders are always short of cash.

On the way home that night, my mind churned with ideas, as Vivian and I walked hand-in-hand in the warm summer breeze. I stopped and turned to her. "Vivian, how would you feel if I gave them the money? Would it be okay?"

She smiled. "That would be terrific! But where are you going to get it?"

"I tell you what I was just thinking," I said. "I don't normally deal with City Bank, but Daytop does. How about if I give City Bank a note for $100,000 and pay them out over a year. They can give the money to Daytop, and the expansion will start right away."

In order to raise more money for Daytop, Vivian produced several fundraising shows called Broadway Salutes Daytop. Fran and Barry Weissler, producers, who were not as successful and famous as they are now, were very helpful and charitable in getting us top entertainers for the shows. Even though the Weisslers are now considered two of the foremost Broadway producers, they have never lost their sense of giving.

The following morning, I met with Monsignor O'Brien to make the offer, and he accepted.

Our association with Daytop Village taught Vivian and I about drug problems in this country. Though our work with the parents association, we now help others to learn. There is no point in a boy or girl graduating from the Daytop program to return home if their parents haven't been educated and the home situation hasn't changed. Parents have to learn what their drug addicted children need, even if those lessons are hard. During the weekly meetings, Daytop instructs parents in how to get their children into the treatment program and what follow-up care is required. One of the best ways they can help is through "tough love." Daytop advocates that parents use tough love to throw their drug addicted children out of the house, to *not* enable their drug use by giving them a nickel, not even for food. The kids must be faced with no alternatives; they need to know that entering the program at Daytop, and graduating from it, is the most loving help their parents can give them. Even today, I continue to assist boys and girls to get into this program because I know it works; I've seen the results.

This program is now thirty-seven years old, and I have spent the past twenty-five years working with it. Much of Daytop's staff is made up of former drug addicts, people who really understand the kids and are committed to helping them. It is a difficult job, and I commend the staff--particularly Brian Madden, Richie Falzone, and Charlie Devlin--for all their efforts. They have saved thousands of lives to date. I believe with all my heart that no child should ever take drugs, but sadly, statistics show that most boys and girls will try them at some point in their lives. I believe the answer to the problem lies in education and treatment, rather than incarceration for juvenile offenders.

Daytop Village has spread through many countries. For instance, there was a serious drug problem among young people in Italy, where drugs were too readily available. Now the treatment centers in Italy are some of our most successful.

My association with this worthy cause has been rewarding in many ways, not the least of which has been the people I've met. Through Monsignor O'Brien, I was invited to the Vatican several times and had the honor of meeting Pope John Paul I, just ten days before he died, and later, Pope John Paul II.

I met Pope John Paul I when he presented Daytop Village with two houses in which to open treatment centers outside Castelgandolfo, the Pope's summer residence in the country. We brought staff over from New York to help set up the new houses and start the programs. We now have more programs operating in Europe and the Far East.

When I had the opportunity to meet Pope John Paul II, we were in the process of splitting our partnership and auctioning off our holdings. I had the best reason in the world for postponing that all-important auction--even Ike understood--I was going to the Vatican for an audience with the Pope.

Vivian and I were invited to join Pope John Paul II for breakfast at 7:00 am. We were picked up by car in Rome and driven to Castelgandolfo, which was quite a ride. Castelgandolfo is a large, beautiful, well-manicured estate on the outskirts of a little village outside Rome, about an hour and a half away. The Pope lives there, along with his usual staff, guards, and nuns.

At first, they wouldn't open the doors and let us into the tremendous courtyard because the Pope was out there jogging, so we had to wait. There were about ten people having breakfast with the Pope that morning in his large dining room, including Monsignor O'Brien, the actress Mary Tyler Moore, her parents, and some other people connected with Daytop, along with two priests.

After breakfast, Monsignor O'Brian and the Pope conducted Mass in the large courtyard, also attended by about twenty nuns. Just before he started the services, the Pope asked his guards to open the gates and let in the boys and girls outside, which they did. Now there were about fifty people seated in the courtyard. Vivian and I sat in the front row and took pictures of the awe-inspiring event. She later pointed out that the Pope was wearing Gucci shoes under his robe.

After the services, the Pope offered communion to anyone who wanted it, and a line formed in front of him. When I jumped up to join it, Vivian asked me where I was going. "I'm going to get communion," I said.

"Nat, you're crazy. You're Jewish, you can't get communion."

I stood in the line anyway, and when the Pope came to me with the wafer, I spoke up. "Your Eminence, before you give me communion, I want to let you know I'm Jewish."

He said, "So is Christ."

And Pope John Paul II gave me communion.

28

Chauffeur, Secretary, and Other Fine Employees

Vivian talked me into hiring a chauffeur because she was worried I might kill myself driving a car while I was tired and working so hard. In my business, I drove all day from job site to job site, leaving the house at 7:00 am and not returning until 7:00 or 8:00 pm. I had employed three other chauffeurs--two who were ex-cops--before Tom Cambria joined me. After more than thirty-one years, he is still my chauffeur.

An experienced chauffeur, Tom is a stocky, good-looking man with a broad chest. I'll never forget that first night he worked for me, the first night of the poker game. When he dropped me off, I told him, "I'll be playing cards and shooting craps until after midnight, so instead of sitting here waiting for me the whole time, why don't you go have dinner and come back."

About two in the morning, when the game was over, I walked out to the car and found my newly-hired chauffeur asleep in the driver's seat. I knocked on the window. "Tom, Tom, wake up, you're sleeping."

Tom's head jerked up. "No, Mr. Serota, I wasn't sleeping. I was meditating."

I have two limousines--a special Lincoln stretch limousine that I've had for many years and the most beautiful Rolls Royce limousine ever built. My Rolls was built in 1965.

I quickly discovered I liked having a chauffeur because it freed me up to do paperwork in the car. Now that cars have phones, I'm on the God-damned phone all the time. I object to car phones, but they are a necessary part of doing business these days.

Over the years, Tom and I have become good friends. On a daily basis I actually spend more time with him than I do with my wife. Tom is tremendously loyal and trustworthy. Practically a member of the family, he was there for me during the good times and the bad, through all the things that went on in my family. He was there when I married Vivian, a woman with three little kids. He was there when Dena died and when Fay died. When I got sick near the end of 1999, Tom stayed with me for ten days and cooked dinner every night.

I hired Tom when I lived in New Jersey, and he still lives there, driving to New York to get me every day. His day is longer than mine; he works harder, time-wise, than I do, and he is invaluable to me. Tom is a very good, very likable man, who takes good care of me. He also never lets me forget what I said to him when I interviewed him for the job.

He'd responded to an ad I'd placed in the paper after I'd fired the last of my ex-cop chauffeurs. "If I hire you," I told Tom then, "you'll have to take a bath every morning before you come to work and put on a clean shirt and tie. I don't want a chauffeur who smells."

These days, I'm always after Tom about his slow, overly careful driving. I get upset and yell at him a lot--that's how I am, and I really haven't got the patience for his driving anymore. And anyway, I'm the boss--me, Serota! I yell like a crazy man, "Tom, I'm in a hurry, step on the God-damned gas!"

All day long it's "Tom do this" and "Tom do that." Even today, I still yell at Tom all the time. After more than thirty years, he's used to it and tosses it out of his mind. He just thinks the crazy man in the back is screaming his head off again--nothing unusual. I admire Tom Cambria. It takes someone with a great strength of character to know when yelling is not being aimed at him personally.

In fact, Tom becomes concerned when I don't yell at him. "Mr. Serota, you're not feeling well today? What's the matter, you're not yelling."

Another special jewel in my life who understood and forgave my gruff ways was my secretary, Claire Leiberman. She worked for me for twenty-five years, and I don't think I fully appreciated her for the first fifteen. She was left-handed, and I thought she was a lousy typist. As much as I would yell at her and insist she do things my way, she'd always let it go and performed her tasks properly and efficiently. Like Tom, she somehow understood that if I called her stupid or yelled, it was not meant personally. I wish to take this moment here and now to apologize for my abusive behavior. I made mistakes, Claire, and I hope you forgive me.

After all those years as my secretary, she was able to read me pretty well. She could sense if I was in a bad mood and would tell the contractors who wanted to see me to come back later. Claire was always concerned about me. She was aware that I went through hell and high water many times, and she was always there for me. I'm grateful for that.

Claire was gentle, and one of her greatest strengths was her ability to care for others. She cared for her mother who had Alzheimer's and spent ten years visiting her in a home. Every day on her way home from work, she brought her mother food, even after her mother stopped recognizing her. Her mother finally passed away at the age of ninety.

In 1999, Claire and her good-looking husband, Stan, bought a home in Florida and retired. I have a new secretary now, but nobody will ever be like Claire. I genuinely miss her.

One of the greatest men who ever worked for me was my first (and only at the time) construction superintendent, Bob Longworth. His son, Roy Longworth, is now my head construction superintendent, extending the family legacy of superior job performance. I owe a great deal of my early success in construction to Bob, who worked with me for thirty-seven years, and my continuing success to Roy, who has now been with me for well over twenty-five years.

Another of the key employees in my company, *Nathan L. Serota and Sons*, is Bert Seelig, who has been with me for the past seventeen or eighteen years. Bert is an architect, engineer, and all-around genius. Bert and I compliment each other and work well together. Anne-Marie DeStefano is a talented secretary who works primarily with Bert and is a big help to him.

In the last couple of years, another important person has joined me, Joe Scimone, a former banker, who is now my chief financial officer. I met Joe when he was in charge of real estate at Fleet Bank. I was so impressed by his smart, no-nonsense, straight-talking style that I asked him to come aboard. It took me quite a few years, but I finally convinced him, and he's doing an excellent job. Steve Appas was hired basically as an accounts receivable man, and he developed into one of my top renting personnel. Peter Aebisher has been with me over twenty years and is now head of maintenance, a very important position, since he oversees all the maintenance for our large number of shopping centers. Tom Whistlehoff, the engineer in my main office building, has been with me from the day the building opened, about twelve years, and he does a fine job coordinating all the building activities.

My office staff are invaluable to me and, despite my gruffness, I treasure them all and know the company wouldn't run smoothly without them. My talented and exceptionally calm head bookkeeper is Terri Ragan, who has been with me for eighteen years. She is aided by equally excellent bookkeepers, the charming Vicky Vargas and the ever-reliable Paula Loeb.

My employees put up with a lot from me sometimes, but we have a good time, and everyone works well together. They have helped me tremendously, and I appreciate that, probably more than they know. I hope some of the expressions they've heard me use over the years will bring a chuckle.

Top 36 Sayings of Nat Serota

1. I know I'm *right*, that's my name.
2. What are you, deaf!
3. Stay home, I'll send the check in the mail.
4. What do you think, money grows on trees?
5. Where is the change?
6. Is Claire in the bathroom, *again*?
7. Claire, get a hearing aid.
8. You're worse than a wife!
9. Let's go, *let's go*!
10. Step on the gas!
11. I hired you to drive, not think!
12. Tom, get over to the right!
13. Do you know how many people I support?
14. Are you *ready*!
15. Private phone calls *again*.
16. I am not working for the phone company.
17. I have to work this weekend so I can pay the salaries.
18. Pick any of the following: Schmuck with earlaps! You moron bastard! You lying bastard! None of your f--king business! Go f--k yourself! Do you need a f-----g hearing aid?
19. Is anybody working today?
20. Who didn't come to work today?
21. What are you, sick *again*?
22. When I'm sick, I come to work.
23. All you think about is eating.
24. Nobody shuts the lights off.
25. What am I, made of money?
26. You can't wait till I leave.
27. Late *again*?
28. Half day today?
29. I haven't got time for this.
30. What's doing today?
31. Did you look at my desk?
32. Everybody out! I have a private call.
33. I don't want to hear it again!
34. I'll sue their ass!
35. You will all miss me when I'm gone.

36. So far today, I've done all right. I haven't gossiped, and I haven't lost my temper. I haven't been grumpy, nasty, or selfish. But in a few minutes, God, I'm going to get out of bed, and that is when I'm going to need a lot of help.

29

Close Calls With the Cops

I must admit to being better off with a chauffeur like Tom who drives carefully (but don't tell Tom I said that). There was a time where he left my employ for about five months to open a restaurant, which didn't work out. I decided to drive myself to work in one of my Cadillacs and immediately got picked up for speeding. The following day, I got picked up for speeding *again*. I explained to the cop that I normally had a chauffeur, but he was away, and yes, I admitted, I had been speeding.

"Officer, have a heart," I said. "I got caught yesterday for speeding, too. If you give me a ticket I'm going to lose my license."

Somehow I managed to talk him out of giving me a ticket. Before the cop went back to his car, he gave me a pointed look. "I strongly suggest you have your chauffeur do the driving in the future."

That wasn't the first experience I'd had with cops pulling me over for speeding, or the first time I'd avoided a ticket. After I left Fay, married Vivian and moved to New Jersey, I drove back to Long Island most weekends to spend time with my sons. I was always in a hurry. About nine o'clock one morning, I left New Jersey and headed for Hewlett Harbor, speeding along Queens Boulevard, a big, wide street with little traffic that early on a Sunday. I glanced in my rear view mirror and spotted a motorcycle cop on a side street. I immediately slowed down. Shortly after that, the cop on the motorcycle pulled out and onto Queens Boulevard to come and get me. His lights blinking, he motioned me to pull over.

When I did, he climbed off the bike and strode up to my car. I rolled down my window and heard his big boots clomping on the pavement and the crackle of his leathers as he leaned toward me. With an innocent expression on my face I said, "Yes, officer?"

"Your license," demanded the cop. "You were speeding. You were driving sixty to sixty-five miles an hour."

I pulled my license out of my wallet. "Who said I was driving that fast?"

"I said so," he answered gruffly.

I cleared my throat. "Excuse me officer, you never clocked me at sixty miles an hour."

"I say I did clock you!"

"You're lying," I accused him. "I saw you sitting on a side street waiting for me, and when I saw you, I slowed down. You couldn't possibly have clocked me doing sixty."

"You son-of-a-bitch, you saw me!" The officer handed me back my license, then adjusted the strap on his helmet. "Well, then get the hell out of here, Mr. Serota. The next time I catch you I'll give you a ticket."

I drove away. But wait, hold the phone, this long story isn't over.

Exactly one month later at nine o'clock on another Sunday morning, I was again speeding along Queens Boulevard on my way to Long Island to see my kids. This time another son-of-bitchin' motorcycle cop came out of nowhere and pulled me over. *It was the same guy!*

Chagrined, I said, "Yes, officer, I'm sorry I was speeding. Please don't give me a ticket. Do you remember about four weeks ago you stopped me? I told you you couldn't clock me and you didn't give me a ticket."

The officer grinned--well, perhaps *sneered* is more the word for it. "Oh yeah, I remember you. You son-of-a-bitch, you're speeding again. And this time I got you!" He flipped open his ticket book.

"Have a little heart," I began my plea. "Why do I have to go to court? You don't really want the hassle of going to court, do you? Let's just hold court right here and I'll pay my fine." I gave him twenty bucks, and that was the end of that.

He climbed back on his motorcycle, but not before issuing a stern warning. "Let me tell you, the next time I catch you speeding, you're getting a ticket."

I had a wonderful time, a marvelous life, and a truly magic way with the cops.

Another day, I was riding in the limousine, in a hurry, and totally fed up with Tom's slow driving. "Tom, you never drive fast enough," I yelled. "I've got to meet my wife at one o'clock and I'm late. Pull the hell over and let me drive!"

He pulled over, and I got into the driver's seat. I sped like crazy along the parkway, trying to make up time. Just before the exit where I would turn onto Long Island Expressway and continue through the tunnel to New York where I would then be minutes from meeting Vivian and almost on time, a damn cop pulled me over for speeding.

The cop sat in a radio car alone, clocking speeders on the parkway (they used to have two cops in the radio cars but cut down because of expenses). I pulled over and shot Tom a look that dared him to comment on the situation. He kept silent while I got out of the limo and walked to the radio car.

Humility had worked for me before. "Officer, you're right, I was speeding," I told him. "I have to get over to New York to meet my wife, and I'm late. Please don't give me a ticket. Let me take care of you."

He nodded. "Walk over to that window and drop whatever you want on the seat."

I dropped a bill through the open window.

The officer eyed me. "If my boss comes along while I've got you pulled over, he's going to want to know if I gave you a ticket. I'll tell him no. Now, let's assume he asks you why you didn't get a ticket, what are you going to tell him?"

"I'll tell him I stopped to ask directions to the tunnel," I answered quickly.

"What about the guy in the car with you?"

"Oh, don't worry about him," I said. "He's my chauffeur."

The cop was amused. "If he's your chauffeur, how come he's not driving?"

"Because he's too God-damned slow!"

"Get out of here!" said the cop, waving me away.

After that, I let Tom drive. He showers every morning and jokingly reminds me I didn't want a chauffeur who smells, but nothing was said about one who drives too carefully.

30

You Can Win a Race, But You Can't Beat the Races

Most of my life, I played cards and gambled--even when I worked at the ice plant for two dollars a day. And when I was in the Army without a real income, I regularly played cards for money. After I built the big housing development in Hewlett, Long Island, I became friendly with many of the men who bought homes from me, and about eight of us would get together every Tuesday night for a poker game held at someone's house. I remember clearly the very first time I got together with those guys. It was thirty-one years ago because it was the same day I'd hired my present chauffeur, Tom Cambria. His first duty had been to drive me to the poker game.

I was always a big gambler, not only at cards and craps, but I bet on basketball, football, and baseball games. There was constant action during the baseball season, and I would bet thousands of dollars every day. I remember once betting $50,000 each on two games in the same day. Having suffered a series of big losses, I was desperate to make my money back. That day, Slottlemyre pitched for the Yankees and, amazingly, I won on both those $50,000 games. But that only proves just how cracked I was because I'd laid down $75,000 to win $50,000; the odds were seven and a half to five. You have to be a sick man to do that.

I lost over two million dollars gambling on sports games. Two years into our marriage, Vivian and I had a big fight about my gambling, she insisting I had a problem and I denying it . . . . Two weeks after that, I lost another $50,000, and it got me thinking about what Vivian had said. I came to admit she was right, and I told myself I'd quit gambling, *right after the next game.*

One night Vivian took me to a Gamblers Anonymous meeting. I never went in, but I haven't bet on a ball game in twenty-nine years! I try to pass on what I've learned about the dangers of gambling by telling my grandchildren never to bet. The truth of the matter is that if I was still betting, my children and grandchildren would likely follow that path because of the poor example I'd set. Children often follow their parents' example; it's not what you say, but *what you do.* For instance, my mother and father never smoked, Vivian and I never smoked, and our children don't smoke.

I still love to play cards, but I quit that, too, because I can't play without gambling and, Vivian doesn't approve. The only time Vivian approves is when she consults with her good friend Cherryl Lee Terry (whose married name is Potier), the numerologist and astrologer. I can recall one time I was told that I had to take a top floor off my office building, and people were betting that I wouldn't do it. So Vivian called Cheryl and asked her to read the numbers of what was going to happen in my future. The numbers told her the building would remain six stories, but they didn't tell her how long my court fight would go on to keep it that way. Cheryl was later married in our home to a charming Frenchman, Gerald Potier.

I do still gamble on occasion, but only when I'm at a casino on the French Riviera and bet a very small amount of francs. When I'm in Monte Carlo, I go to the casino to play craps as a "wrong better." A wrong better is rare; he bets against the shooter. Most gamblers bet on the shooter, but I bet with the house--the house says the shooter is going to lose, and I bet that the house is right. I'm better off wagering this way because the odds are better for me. I usually have a system, but I'm not about to spill it here in this book for everyone to learn.

However, let me explain the game of craps for anyone reading who isn't familiar with it. The odds set in a crap game are actually perfect. If the dice is thrown a million times and you mark down the numbers each time, you'd find they have an equal chance of coming up. Craps is a dice game of arithmetic. But most gamblers don't bet that way. To make money as a big gambler, which I used to be, you throw the dice, bet big, and lose plenty before you win.

Gambling, by its very nature, is unpredictable. The word gamble means to win or lose, but the reason gamblers play is because they always think they're going to win. It's fun to win--hell to lose, but fun to win. When I play now, in long betting, I always think I'm going to win, and most times I do win, but not all the time. Sometimes I go crazy and put too much money up, thinking the shooter can't possibly make another number. Then, amazingly, he does . . . and I lose it all. On many occasions, I've seen the person throwing the dice hold the dice (keep winning) for over an hour.

Every once in a while, I go to the horse races in Miami or New York, especially with Monsignor O'Brien, who enjoys the track. He is a special man and a good friend. However, my main form of gambling is my building business. A businessman is always gambling--I buy land and gamble on producing it; clothing manufacturers or match stick makers gamble on whether their product will sell. Back when I built my first two houses, I gambled all the money I had to my name--$3,500 at the time--on whether or not I'd make a profit. I had to convince the bank to lend me the money to gamble with, and I either had to pay it back or declare bankruptcy. It's my opinion that everyone gambles on a daily basis. Gambling in business is a part of life. Businesses fail and people go bankrupt all the time.

Gambling becomes an addiction when you bet more than you can afford to lose. Shooting craps or betting on a ball game that way is idiotic. You can beat the race, but not the racers; you can beat the ball game, but not the game; and you can win one horse race, but you can't win seven out of seven.

31

Fay's Death

As I mentioned, Fay had refused to divorce me, but our marriage was over and I had moved on with my life. I was good to Fay and took good care of her after I left. Although we never made any kind of legal agreement, I gave her the $5,000,000 house and all the money and things she could ever possibly want. When our son, Charles, got married, they held the wedding at the mansion, and it was a huge affair. I bought Fay diamonds for the occasion.

I always loved my first wife in a certain way. It didn't seem odd to me to love two women at the same time. Our separation (divorce in my mind) was difficult for Fay at first. Fay wouldn't give me a divorce in New York State. Not giving me a divorce was her way of hanging on to me, although she understood I had moved on with my life. A few years before her death, she finally gave me the legal divorce, and that's when I married Vivian for the fifth and final time.

In 1991, Fay died in my arms. A smoker when she was younger, she lost a torturous, eight-month battle with lung cancer. She suffered through operations and treatments while the doctors did everything they could to try to save her. She died in Mount Sinai Hospital in New York City. While she was very ill, I visited her regularly, and our sons, Charles and Geoffrey, kept a constant vigil. On the last night, when Fay was in a coma, I sent Geoff over to my place, five minutes away, to take a shower, shave, and have a nap. He hadn't left his mother's side in three days, and I promised I'd stay with her and call him immediately if anything changed.

She woke up, hovered at the edge of awareness while I held her in my arms and spoke to her gently. "Fay, let go. You don't have to hold on anymore." Charles and Geoff both rushed back to the hospital in time to be with their mother when she passed away.

With love in my heart, I held Fay, and she let go.

Life must go on. She'd already let go of me. Now, she had let go of life. I said goodbye to my first love, the first woman I'd married.

32

Believe in Yourself

It's good to have your sons and daughters in business with you. Without my children and grandchildren, I would find no glory in my success, no reason for my tireless efforts, and little meaning to my life's work.

For example: Say you're running a business and you make a good living for yourself and your wife, but you don't have any children. As you grow older, you will inevitably come to a point in your life where you wonder why you worked so hard when you have nobody to leave the results of your efforts to when you're gone.

I was very fortunate to be in a business where I could afford to invite my sons to join me when they finished their education. Charles, Geoffrey, and Daniel all work in the building business with me. I started the business for them, and I hope they will keep it going for their grandchildren as a family legacy.

In any job, an inexperienced worker should expect to have to learn all the facts of a particular business and gain necessary experience before taking on more responsibilities. When a boy goes into business with his father, he should start at the bottom rung, as there is much to learn on the way up. But sometimes the child objects to that. It takes time for a child to grow, and that growth comes through making mistakes. And my children have all made mistakes, as I did in the beginning, and my father before me when he worked for his father.

No two people handle business in the same way, especially fathers and sons. People think differently and approach tasks in a different manner. It is important to learn how to think each task through thoroughly from beginning to end. It is also important to communicate, to ask when you don't know something, to listen to other's suggestions and solutions to problems.

For some people, working hard means simply putting in the time. A man has been with me for a couple of years now, whom I think is fantastic. He works hard but he doesn't work properly (which I anticipated when I hired him). He might be on the phone talking about the possibility of doing business with someone and, certainly, that is working, but it's not working smart. Therein lies the problem.

I'm getting older and my sons handle a lot of the business, each working in his own way, each with his own strengths. They all do well in business, even though they often disagree amongst themselves and with me. My oldest son, Charles, has been working with me for twenty-six years, and we still disagree about the way to handle many basic things involving building or renting and collecting. Many times, I've been in meetings with my three sons where they will each come up with a completely different solution to handle a certain situation. Geoff will go on about one thing, Daniel will talk about something else, and Charles will have a third idea. It can be a problem.

One of the things a father has to do is help his children to understand each other, as well as the business. These days, I try to see myself as working for them and to make my role in the business one of mediator whenever they don't agree. I try to give them the wisdom of my experience by showing them how I would handle it and making them understand the reasons why.

I've learned that working smart means using your head in every respect, whatever you're doing. You should check, double-check, and even triple-check. Don't take anything for granted. I have always believed that two heads are better than one. In my case, I have three sons and believe that three heads are better than one--plus my head--so now that's four heads working together. Even if there is an initial disagreement, ultimately the project shapes up better with everybody sharing all the facts while having different angles of approach to a particular problem. It may make for a lively working environment, but in the end a more successful business.

33

Work or Play, I Enjoyed Every Day

As you may have gathered I work a lot, but I *enjoy* my work. I'm lucky to have a business which still excites and interests me. My work is creatively fulfilling because I get to produce something I think of. I don't buy buildings that are built, rather I buy a piece of land with the dream of creating something on it that is going to make me a living in one fashion or another. I have a vision for the project and enjoy the challenge of making it happen. When I get through, I stand back and look at the building and the land which had nothing on it when I started, and I feel like an artist who has painted a picture or taken a block of stone and molded a statue. Builders create something out of nothing, and that gives me a great deal of satisfaction.

Over the years, as I think this story shows, my work has been important to me, but it has not been the only thing in my life. Granted, I'm very busy and don't have much time for recreation and entertainment. I love to travel with Vivian. We have an apartment in Monaco and we regularly visit France.

Understand one thing: Nat Serota is supposedly a wealthy man, but I like to cut corners when I can. One night at three or four in the morning when I couldn't sleep, I was reading *The New York Times* and came across a full-page ad for Delta Airlines. They were offering round-trip flights to Paris for $228 (off-season). I stared at the ad, thinking of the First Class tickets I usually bought for $6-7,000 per ticket, and came up with an idea. I'd buy three or four seats for myself in the center section and two for Vivian on the window side because she's smaller, then raise the seat rests and stretch out--round-trip tickets; we'd sleep both ways. This proved harder to do than you might think.

I called the airline to make the reservations, had some difficulty with my request to put the same name on several seats, but finally got them. When we went to the airport, we ran into more problems. Nobody had seen this done before and couldn't believe it. They checked and discovered that I had, indeed, paid for all the seats, and they had to give them to me. I did this five or six times, and it always amazed people. One time, an attendant even put a net over the three seats so no one would bother me.

Another way that I cut corners has to do with another good friend of mine, Dr. Marvin King, Associate Professor at the School of Dental and Oral Surgery at Columbia University. He's more than a dentist--he's got a heart too. His specialty is to provide dental care for the handicapped. (His lovely wife, Lorna, was a lead dancer in many Broadway shows.) Marvin has been a dentist for forty years or more, and because of a special deal we've got going, I'm way ahead of the game. Here's the deal: every time he cleans my teeth, we flip a coin to decide who's going to pay. So far, my record is running something like five to two!

Other than traveling, I enjoy listening to music, especially opera. The three big tenors are my favorite: Pavarotti, Carrara, and Placido Domingo. I watch television, and I love the theater. Whenever I visit London, I make a point of seeing a show every night. In New York, I have such a busy social life that I don't get out to the Broadway shows as often as I'd like. I enjoy the many parties and dinners with friends that we attend, but there are times when I'd honestly rather go to a show or stay home and read a book.

I like to read detective and adventure stories. All my life, I've read every night before going to sleep. Unfortunately, my eyesight was recently affected by an accident, and I haven't been able to read since. I had a serious fall on Christmas Eve 1999, and now I have to blink my eyes a lot because my vision goes from light to dark. I really miss reading, and I'm hoping a specialist will be able to fix the problem. There must be about a dozen books waiting on my bedside table that I want to read right now, but I don't have the patience to struggle with my vision problems.

If I were able to do more of what I most enjoyed in life, it would be traveling, going to other countries and experiencing other cultures, knowing other people, and seeing the marvels of geography and history firsthand. I was in China in 1983, and I would really like to travel there again. I wanted to go back immediately, but I never got the chance, and now the China I visited in 1983 doesn't exist. It's hard to decide (if time-travel were possible) whether I'd rather go back and visit China as it was then or see the country as it is today. China is changing radically, and capitalism emerges more and more there, as the old line dies out. That change will be something to witness. I think that Cuba is about to change radically and will become an exciting place to visit after Castro is gone. Havana could well go back to being a gambling center and a big draw for American tourists again. I think this would greatly benefit the Cuban people who have nothing and are suffering terribly.

If I had a chance to live my life over again, I would just enjoy everything in general, as I did this time. I would like to be born all over again, knowing what I know now. I'd like to start with nothing and make it fun. Life is exciting and wonderful, even the struggles. I had to struggle all my life, but I can honestly say I enjoyed every day.

34

Why is My Tombstone in My Office?

Some people find it odd that I have my own tombstone in my office. When I married Vivian, thirty-one years ago, as I mentioned, I was married to two women at that time. Thoughts began swirling in my mind: *What if I drop dead tomorrow? Who's going to bury me, and how will it be done? What if they're fighting over the body?* I decided I'd better take matters into my own hands and make preparations in advance.

Many years earlier, after my father had died and when my mother was ill, I purchased a family plot with twelve graves. I was in the Army and had little money at the time, but I put fifty dollars down toward the three hundred dollars I paid for twelve graves in the new Wallwood Cemetery, near where my father was buried. That price goes to show how land values have increased since then. I later moved my father and he rests beside my mother and other family members. I planned to rest there, too. Except for my tombstone and my eulogy, I was already prepared.

One day, I was out on Long Island and stopped to see one of my building suppliers. Over the course of our conversation, I learned his landlord was Sprung Memorial, in the building next door. Sprung Memorial is well-known for making and planting tombstones. I had an immediate brainstorm and told my friend I needed to go and buy a footstone.

"Did someone die?" he asked.

"No, I want to buy it for myself." I proceeded to explain.

At first he thought I was kidding, but when he learned I was serious, he shook his head in amusement and introduced me to Mr. Sprung. I told him I wanted to order a granite footstone.

Mr. Sprung nodded solemnly and started to write up the order. "Who is the stone for?" he asked in that gentle voice reserved for dealing with bereaved customers.

"Me."

"What?" he said incredulously, quickly losing his somber manner. "But I've never made a stone for anyone who was alive."

"Well, you are now. And I want it wholesale."

We settled on $175 (a very good deal), and he agreed to add my date of death when the time came. I pulled the cash out of my pocket and paid him on the spot.

"What am I supposed to do with the stone in the meantime?" Mr. Strung asked.

"Deliver it to my office," I replied, then I convinced him to include a flat piece of granite for the footstone to sit on.

Six months later, my receptionist, Ruth, walked into my office to announce that a monument truck had arrived with a delivery. I told her not to say anything to anyone and have the truck drive around back to unload. I met the two men and watched them put the tombstone on a trolley and wheel it into my office. I planted it next to my desk.

Prior to that, I had installed new carpet in my office and purposely chosen green like grass in anticipation of the arrival of the stone. You should have seen the looks on the employees' faces when they saw it. The stone now sits in a prime location in the new, large, beautiful office I recently built for myself--against the wall, next to the piano.

I was almost prepared--only one more thing left to do. I picked up the phone and called Monsignor William O'Brien. As I mentioned earlier, I had served as chairman of the board for eleven years for Daytop Village. I knew the Monsignor wrote obituaries for departed people associated with Daytop because he always called to tell me whenever they appeared in *The New York Times*. I'd been reading them for years and now wanted him to prepare *my* obituary, so I could read it *before* I died.

He agreed to do it. Five to seven years went by, and every time I talked to the Monsignor, I reminded him about writing my obituary. He claimed he had a funny one and a good one in the works, but I never saw anything. On November 6, 1999, I underwent a heart valve operation in Boston. Shortly after my operation, I received a call from the Monsignor at the hotel where I was recuperating, staying nearby to make sure nothing happened before I made the trip back to New York. He flew to Boston to see me for lunch the next day.

"I brought you a present," he told me, handing me the completed obituary.

I am pleased to be able to include it in this chapter.

Obituary for Nathan L. Serota

Upon gazing on The Parthenon, The Pyramids, The Taj Mahal *and* The Great Cathedrals, *I have often wondered as to what "Great Passion" conceived and actualized such incredible treasures at the outer limits of man's creative spirit. And closer to home, the indomitable Robert Moses enjoyed my childhood fantasies with near godly powers to hurl great steel wonders across gaping chasms of rushing waters. A Builder, indeed, ranks among Heaven's blessed, pushing back in each generation the perimeters of man's creations. Nat Serota, my Friend, is numbered among "This Tribe." While Robert Frost in his* Mending Wall *begged the central question for the Master Builder: "Before I build a wall, I'd ask to know! What I was walling in or walling out!", Nat, just a 'City Kid' who manned the coal chutes and the ice blocks of yesteryear, dreamed this 'Builder's Dream' of creating wonderlands for the teeming masses emigrating to the wide expanses of suburbia. Bright and imaginative in design, these bore the 'Serota Stamp' of inclusiveness, and overnight became the great people-gathering places: shopping arcades, theaters, housing, recreation meccas for the young, pleasant settings for the elderly. And all the while, he lent his limitless energies to building 'new tomorrows' for the young people of Daytop Village for over a quarter century--his quintessential building mission. Heaven has a special claim upon "His Tribe." We have been immensely enriched by his life--and immeasurably diminished by his passing. Our prayerful support for his beloved Vivian and his Family.*

Monsignor William B. O'Brien
President, Daytop Village, Inc.

35

Secrets of a Good Marriage

Vivian and I traveled all over the world during our marriage and still enjoy travel together. Nurit Kahane Haase has been helping us with our travel plans for over twenty years. She's the only good travel agent I've ever had and a friend, too. Stella Rosenstein is her adorable assistant who never complains, no matter how many times I change my tickets.

In recent years, we've enjoyed traveling to Ascot in June with Louise and Steven Kornfeld. Vivian met Louise through the vivacious Ivana Trump at one of Ivana's chic luncheons. Steven is an adventurous and worldly man who spends more time in the air than on the ground. They're a very caring and considerate couple, and I'm happy they are our friends.

The whole family spent every summer in Europe. I still ran my business then, so I'd spend two weeks vacationing with them, then return to work in New York for a week, then go back to Europe for two weeks, alternating that way all summer. I always took the Concorde from Paris to New York, where it landed at eight-thirty. My chauffeur promptly picked me up in my limo and, within ten minutes, I arrived at my office where I'd work straight through for twenty-two hours before sleeping. The following Friday, I'd take the overnight flight directly to Nice where Vivian picked me up the next morning. I had a car and a boat in

Monte Carlo, and we'd spend the next two weeks there, then go home for a week or two unless something else came up. Our summers in Europe were great, and even though I'm getting on in years now, Vivian and I continue to visit Paris every summer, the place we first fell in love.

On one of our early trips to France, we saw a gorgeous woman dressed in white at the Hotel L'Voil D'or that we were staying at. She turned out to be Phyllis Trenk, wife of Al Trenk. They were very much in love and truly adored each other. In fact, they were high school sweethearts. They became our dearest friends. And over the course of twenty-six years, we travelled to France together every summer. They lived in New Jersey, had an apartment in Manhattan, and a house in the Hamptons, so we saw them often. Vivian and Phyllis were devoted friends. As soul sisters, they really knew each other and would talk about things they'd never tell another about their life, not even their husbands.

Al is a true friend and a wonderful guy with a great sense of humor, only rivaled by his great sense of direction. Phyllis was a terrific lady: beautiful but not vain, determined but not bossy. She could tell me off and I would take it from her. The four of us always had a good time with never an angry word. We bought a boat together in France, a beautiful thirty-foot Offshorer, a fast speedboat. We'd go to Portofino, St. Tropez, Cannes--stop to swim in the ocean and enjoy the sun along the way.

We were desolate when Phyllis died a few years ago from lung cancer. Al was determined to find the right doctors to save her and did everything in his power to keep her alive. She showed us how to die with grace, still caring about others' needs. Phyllis never forgot a birthday or an anniversary, and a week before she died, she remembered to send the little boy next door a birthday card. To some of her friends, she sent a flowering tree so that every spring now the memory of Phyllis is kept alive not only in our hearts, but in the fragrance and beauty of those blossoms for all to see.

During the summers we spent with them in France and Italy, there were many interesting people who crossed our path and whose friendship we still enjoy. To name a few: Joyce Dana and Bob Glaser; Susie Reeves; Lois and Buzz Aldrin; Lady Lavinia Samuel; Toni and Martin Sassnoff; Senior Carmen Gumina; Lily Sada; Richard Irving; Nicky and Terrance Cole; Liz Bruer, Sigrid and Burt Axelrad; Bunny and Jeff Dell; James and Simira Speno; the Castragnas: Bianco, Franco, and Max, their son; and Gilda and James Gourley.

I believe in marriage. It makes me very happy to come home every day to find my wife there. I enjoy being with her, speaking with her, living *completely with her*, and getting and giving full support. And I love Vivian.

The advice my mother gave me about marriage was: "Before you marry a girl or tell her you want to marry her, look at her mother, because most girls will turn out like their mothers." I think that is the truth, and I told my sons, "Don't get yourself excited because the girl is very beautiful and sweet today. Go see their mother first."

What makes a successful marriage is really the commitment and respect you have for one another, the soul support. You try to keep that respect during the marriage by not taking advantage of one another. Whatever decision comes up, don't make it for yourself alone. Marriage is a partnership. Always find out how the other party feels about it.

I have seen it--felt it--many times, when a situation arises, one spouse will say the decision is terrific, but the other spouse doesn't think it's so great. Both should agree on a decision, otherwise a major problem is created. Partners have to talk it through. On occasion, I've experienced this personally with both of my spouses and my children, and learned not to look at decisions as if I was the only one to benefit. I ask myself if the other person is suffering. Will he or she have to work harder for the particular change in life I want to make? It can be hard to focus on the needs of someone else when you're trying to succeed at your own goals.

To make a marriage work, it is important for each partner to think of the other's feelings and concerns, and consider how the consequences of an action might affect the other before you take it. This is not only the key to success in marriage, but to success in all relationships. I sit down with my children and talk things through, and I do the same with my employees. If you are going to make a deal, the deal must benefit both. It has to be win-win, or otherwise forget it, because it won't work.

Why has our marriage succeeded all these years? Vivian and I are deeply involved with each other; we're integral parts of the fabric of each other's lives, and we truly *know* each other. Kids who live together in college for four or five years and then get married are often soon divorced. They end up taking everything for granted and losing respect for each other. The man thinks that when his girlfriend becomes his wife she has to take care of him, wash the dishes and cook for him, etc. Before they were married and he took her out to dinner, the girlfriend, out of deference to him, would not choose the most expensive item on the menu. When it's her boyfriend who is picking up the check, she is more respectful and courteous, but when they're married, she sees the money as theirs, not just his, so she figures she can have a lobster or a steak. In my opinion, both of these views are wrong, and they create problems in marriage. I believe, sincerely, that you have to live with a person before you can really know them. I'm not talking about "living together."

I mentioned earlier that I couldn't wait to get home every night to be with my wife and that we talk on the phone a lot during the day. When I asked Vivian how many times a day we talk, she said gently, "A lot more when you're cranky or miserable."

And I have to agree that I am often cranky these days.

36

Children and Grandchildren

At the time of this writing, I have two granddaughters and five grandsons. Jennifer (twenty-three) and Lauren (twenty) are the daughters of Charles and his pretty wife, Karen. Both granddaughters are beautiful and brilliant.

Jennifer does computer work and design; she graduated from Syracuse, one of the top students in her class. She's sharp and creative. On her first venture into the job market, she secured an excellent position with a big salary, making designs for various corporate entities.

Lauren is a gifted writer and poet. She's worked in London, written for a newspaper, and traveled in Europe and Asia. A brilliant student, she currently attends Sarah Lawrence in a writing program and, I'm quite certain, her creative talents and fortitude will take her where she wants to go in life.

From my thirty-one year marriage to Vivian, I have two additional children, Deborah who was sensitive and volatile as a child, but who grew to be a loving, lovely, young woman, and Daniel. Deborah married Kenneth Carbone, a successful restaurateur, a super husband, and a hands-on father. They have two clever sons, Michael (nine) and James (four). Michael is tall and good-looking, fun, loves to tell jokes, and is already a talented basketball player. James is another good-looking kid, full of positive energy and determination, who's always telling me that he wants to be the boss.

Daniel was two years old when I married Vivian, so I raised him, and therefore, he's terrific. He is now a successful builder and married to a stunning gal, Cherie. Cherie's got a thriving business of her own called Belly Basics. She designs and sells chic clothes for pregnant women. Together, they're doing a great job of raising their three handsome, intelligent sons who will carry on the Serota name: Stephen (eight), Jonathan (five), and Chase (twenty months). Steve is a good student, a gifted ice-hockey player, and a real "dealmaker" when he wants something; he doesn't just ask, he negotiates. Jonathan is a take-charge kid, showing early signs of musical talent as a singer, and he's crazy about karate. And little Chase is a charmer who loves to bang on the drums.

37

The World According to Serota

"Don't put your dreams on hold" is a saying I lived by, and reflecting on my life now, I realize I have made most of my dreams come true. I told my story in this book because I want my children and grandchildren to understand the important things in life--honesty, honor, and being good to others. I have striven to live my life *without hurting anyone.*

The best advice I could leave behind for my grandchildren is: Always remember you can do anything you want to do. Make up your mind to do it, work at it, and you will succeed. **Don't put your dreams on hold.**

In living your life, you will reach that fork in the road where a left turn might take you away from the security of making a living, while the right turn might take you one step closer to conquering your dream. If you have to supply money to your family--your mother, father, children--if you are in that situation, as I was, then you have responsibility for others, and your primary goal is to make money. If you are only supporting yourself and have no one else to consider, I think you should take the fork to the right, follow your dreams, and conquer what you truly want in life. Be creative and make something of *yourself* instead of just making money.

Don't waste time; you can't recover time you've wasted. Actively chase your dream as fast as possible to attain your goals. If you are doing something you *don't* enjoy, that is a waste of time, and once time is gone, it's gone.

If you're not happy with yourself, money wont make you happy. If you earn money just to buy material things, they won't buy you happiness. I have tried to pass on to my kids what I've learned from my own experience. When I used to work for the railroad and traveled down south with my pass, I would look out the train windows and study life as it went by. I'd see people living in little shacks along the track--a guy sitting in his rocking chair with a smile on his face, contentedly smoking a corncob pipe. I realized that the man sitting in front of that little shack was doing something that made him happy. He didn't have to be rich to be happy. It's liking yourself that gives you happiness, not wealth; wealth is transient.

To follow your dreams, you must have the courage to climb the mountains required to achieve your dreams and to believe you can do it.

In addition to building and creating, loving and doing for others makes me happy. The old adage of it being "better to give than receive" happens to be true. I remember when I worked for the railroad and someone gave me a gratuity of a dollar or two, it felt very good, but what feels even better to me now is to turn that around and give it back in another way, now that I have the resources to do so. Today, I am fortunate to have a few dollars, and what makes me feel best is to share those dollars with someone else. I love to give money away.

Daytop Village has a saying: "You can't keep it unless you give it away." If you think about that saying, it rings true. If you give something away, the good Lord returns it to you in another fashion. What good is having wealth unless you give it away? Why leave money sitting in your bank account when it can do someone else a lot of good, and in so doing, bring happiness to yourself at the same time?

Some people have tried to tell me not to give my money away, but it gives me a lot of pleasure to give money away. I've been giving it away for years. As I made my way through life, I came in contact with all kinds of people and often found myself in a position to help them. I have a deal where I just recently signed a mortgage for a young couple I know who needed help. They had a problem getting a mortgage, so I phoned the bank and guaranteed it.

Some of the good people I met over the years needed me. One of those was Ben Tannhauser. He and his partner, Brown, were brokers in the theater business; they arranged the rental of theaters to movie companies for a fee. Many of the shopping centers I built had theaters in them, and the two elderly brokers regularly brought me tenants. Eventually Brown died, and Tannhauser remained in the business, continuing to deal with me. Ben was a wonderful human being, and we became good friends. His wife, Juliet, was very beautiful and had been a show girl in her youth. They had no children and lived in Oceanside, about fifteen minutes from my office, with their dog, Peppe.

One morning, when Ben was getting on in years, he came to my office for breakfast, and I noticed he had difficulty swallowing. He told me he had cancer. At the time, I owed him $25,000 on a deal we had put together, so I offered to pay him outright then. He didn't handle money well and wanted to take what he needed in smaller amounts, rather than a lump sum. I agreed to pay him in that fashion and promised that, if he died, I would make sure Juliet got the rest of the money. Amazingly, he beat the cancer in his eighties and lived on for many more years until he was completely broke.

Juliet died before he did. By that time, I had paid Ben out, but he had spent all the money; he had nothing left to bury his wife. I bought two cemetery plots, near where I'm going to lay, chose and paid for a lovely casket, and buried Juliet. Ben kept the home in Oceanside (the only thing he still owned) and continued to live there while I gave him money every month, and Claire and Tom checked on him and delivered food. He had no one. We took care of him until he died, and I buried him in the plot next to Juliet, the little dog between them.

After Ben died, his will was read, and I discovered he'd left his house to me--some of the proceeds going to Tom and Claire, and the remainder, he'd written, was to pay back all the money he felt he owed me. He died with no family around him and had left his belongings to me, including several two dollar bills which I still have.

Sometimes giving money away is good business. Forty years ago, I built a shopping center, and the library in the area wanted to open a new facility. They didn't have much money, so they rented space from me for a public library in the shopping center, telling me they wanted to build their own larger building when they had raised the funds. Three years later, they had the money, and I donated some extra land beside the shopping center for them to build on. It was a smart business move because I knew hundreds of parents would come each week to drop their kids off at the Shirley Town Library, then go to the shopping center. It's a gorgeous library, and my picture still hangs on the wall.

Daniel is always on the lookout for a project he can build on his own. Recently, he found a piece of property belonging to New York Technical University on Long Island. It cost six million dollars for ten beautiful five-acre plots on which Daniel could build ten luxury homes. The property is excellent, but six million is not chicken feed. We decided to buy it, and right then, New York Tech hit me over the head for a million dollar donation. They offered to put my name on their new medical building, but I had no use for that. However, I gladly donated the money (yet another good business move), and they named the medical school's new teaching facility after my parents, *Hannah and Charles Serota*. There the students are taught how to do autopsies. Daniel and I toured the new building and were shocked at the sight of a large number of gruesome, dismembered bodies on slabs inside, but the doctors of tomorrow have to learn somewhere.

I like to give money to panhandlers in New York City where I live. I often hand money out to starving people on the sidewalk, even though some of them are on drugs or may have other problems. Vivian thinks it's too dangerous for an eighty-one year old man to walk along the streets of New York shelling out money to down-and-out strangers. One chilly winter evening, we were walking briskly back from dinner when I noticed a man digging in the trash can. I stopped and turned back. "Vivian, I'm going back to that man," She urged me not to take the risk, but I persisted. I walked back to the man, pulled out a twenty dollar bill and gave it to him. He threw it into the trash basket, thus proving his mental deficiency.

Sadly, many of the homeless are mentally ill. I believe that many of the murders we read about in the newspapers every day--not premeditated murder or spousal abuse--are committed by people who are mentally ill. I don't think those killers belong in the electric chair; they should be taken care of because they are ill. But I suppose that is the basis of Vivian's point: that there *are* mentally ill and dangerous people in need on the streets of New York City, and I should be more careful.

There are some difficulties shared by different races throughout the world, and I don't believe that we, as affluent white Americans, share enough of our good fortune with the underprivileged. We have the world by the balls. We get up every morning with a roof over our heads and food to eat. We have opportunity in this country. There is a whole world out there that doesn't even have a *sense* of opportunity. That is a crime.

If I were born again, I'd like to see better things happen in the world. When I look at countries such as India, or parts of Africa where AIDS is rapidly spreading, or other third world countries, I wish I could come back and earn *really* big money in order to pass it on.

There are many problems in the world, and the drug problem compounds all the others. I believe the dealers are responsible for the drug problem. I don't mean the poor kids selling drugs in the street or the guy who brings in a couple of thousand dollars worth. I'm talking about the big guys, the *really big guys* bringing it in from other countries.

Monsignor O'Brien and I talk at length on these subjects. Once I suggested we go to Congress and lobby for the execution of the big drug lords from other countries who bring drugs into America. The Monsignor told me he couldn't go along with that. "I'm a priest, a man of the cloth," he said. "I don't believe we should kill them."

I still say that if five or ten of these guys were executed every year, we'd soon see the drug problem cease. They wouldn't be so willing to risk bringing drugs into this country anymore if the crime was punishable by death.

So, how do we cure the sins that exist in this world? This question puzzles me, and I get pretty disturbed over it. There is so much suffering and so many problems in the world that, at times, I doubt there is a God. I say to my Rabbi, Preacher, Indian Chief: "Show me where God is. Look at that child who is blind; look at that woman who is starving; look at that man who is blind. And show me where God is."

I say it to Vivian, who is religious, and she tells me, "He's not a personal God, he can't watch everything, Nat." Some days, I do believe in God. I don't really pray, but I look around and I see the good in life and think perhaps it wouldn't exist without God. Don't get me wrong, I'm grateful for my success. But at times, I wonder, why me? Why is it that Nat Serota was smart enough to make all this money? Why me and not someone else? I've been lucky enough to enjoy a big life.

38

Final Thoughts

My feeling is that everybody should be entitled to the good things in life. However, having the good things in life doesn't necessarily mean having dollars. It could mean having good health or good feelings toward others. To me, having the good things in life means the joy of meeting someone you fall in love with, having children to take care of and love, and who love you. This is the part of life that is wonderful and delicious. This is the part that made me want to savor every moment.

Giving to another human being gives me a great deal of pleasure. I'm not talking about monetary giving. I'm talking about caring about someone else and having them care about you. I'm talking about having the will to make the other person satisfied, to give them happiness and make them feel cared for. This is most important.

My near-fatal accident gave me pause to think about life and death. I've come to the conclusion that the person left alive who cared for the one who dies must realize that the dead person is now sleeping. Don't feel bad for him, because there is no pain in death. He is not missing life because he is sleeping and no longer exists. I understand more about death since this happened to me. I had absolutely no awareness of collapsing. I was in the hospital for ten days before I even realized I was in the hospital.

My point is that I want my loved ones to know this and not be concerned about me when I die. Through this book, I leave a final message for you, my loved ones: Please don't cry for me. I'm fine now. I only want you to understand that I love you.

In my life, I always wanted to give you as much as I could, and now I want you to do the same for me. You can't keep it unless you give it away. I want you to love others and give to others. By loving and giving, you have the ability to make someone else happy.